1st Workshop on Post-Editing in Modern-Day Translation 2020

Held at AMTA 2020

Online
6 – 9 October 2020

ISBN: 978-1-7138-2376-6

The 14th Conference of
The Association for Machine Translation
in the Americas

www.amtaweb.org

WORKSHOP PROCEEDING

1st Workshop on Post-Editing in Modern-Day Translation

Organizers:
John E. Ortega (Universitat d'Alacant and New York University)
Marcello Federico (Amazon)
Constantin Orasan (University of Surrey)
Maja Popovic (ADAPT Centre)

Organizers

John E. Ortega (Universitat d'Alacant and New York University): jeo10@alu.ua.es
Marcello Federico (Amazon): marcfede@amazon.com
Constantin Orasan (University of Surrey): c.orasan@surrey.ac.uk
Maja Popovic (ADAPT Centre): maja.popovic@adaptcentre.ie

Program Committee

Lucia Specia (Imperial College London)
Maja Popovic (ADAPT Centre)
Kyunghyun Cho (New York University)
Daniel Torregrosa (World Intellectual Property Organization)
Nora Aranberri (Universidad del País Vasco)
Alberto Poncelas (ADAPT Centre)
Barry Haddow (University of Edinburgh)
Sheila Castilho (Dublin City University)
Constantin Orasan (University of Surrey)
Sharon O'Brien (ADAPT Centre)
John Moran (Transpiral)
Carlos Teixeira (IOTA and Trinity College Dublin)
Antonio Toral (University of Groningen)
Rohit Gupta (Apple)
Patrick Simianer (Lilt)
José Guilherme Camargo de Souza (eBay Inc.)
Michel Simard (National Research Council Canada)
Marco Turchi (Fondazione Bruno Kessler)
Matteo Negri (Fondazione Bruno Kessler)
Marcello Federico (Amazon)
Jeffrey Killman (University of North Carolina at Charlotte)
Alina Karakanta (Fondazione Bruno Kessler)
Miquel Esplà Gomis (Universitat d'Alacant)
Diego Bartolome (Transperfect)
Marcin Junczys-Dowmunt (Microsoft)
Kevin Knight (DiDi Labs)
Nicola Ueffing (eBay Inc.)
Alon Lavie (Unbabel)
Isabel Lacruz (Kent State University)
Adam Meyers (New York University)
Tsz Kin Lam (Heidelberg University)
Rebecca Knowles (National Research Council Canada)

Contents

Evaluating MT based on translation speed -

a review of the status quo and a proposal for the future

John Moran

Proceedings of the 14th Conference of the Association for Machine Translation in the Americas
October 6 - 9, 2020, 1st Workshop on Post-Editing in Modern-Day Translation

Overview

- Q&A
- 8 years ago (iOmegaT)
- The last 8 years (MTPE in Transpiral)
- The next few years

Proceedings of the 14th Conference of the Association for Machine Translation in the Americas
October 6 - 9, 2020, 1st Workshop on Post-Editing in Modern-Day Translation

Some (historical background)

Mirko Plitt, François Masselot. A Productivity Test of Statistical Machine Translation Post-Editing in a Typical Localisation Context. The Prague Bulletin of Mathematical Linguistics No. 93, 2010, pp. 7-16. ISBN 978-80-904175-4-0. doi: 10.2478/v10108-010-0010-x.

144,648 source words processed – PE was 43% faster

"*Figure 4 shows a comparison between post-editing throughput and edit distance. One could intuitively expect that fast translators make fewer changes than slow translators. In our test, however, the post-editor who made the highest number of changes was also the fastest. The graphs indicate no clear correlation between edit distance and throughput.*"

So beware of using ONLY edit distance for PE pricing

Proceedings of the 14th Conference of the Association for Machine Translation in the Americas
October 6 - 9, 2020, 1st Workshop on Post-Editing in Modern-Day Translation

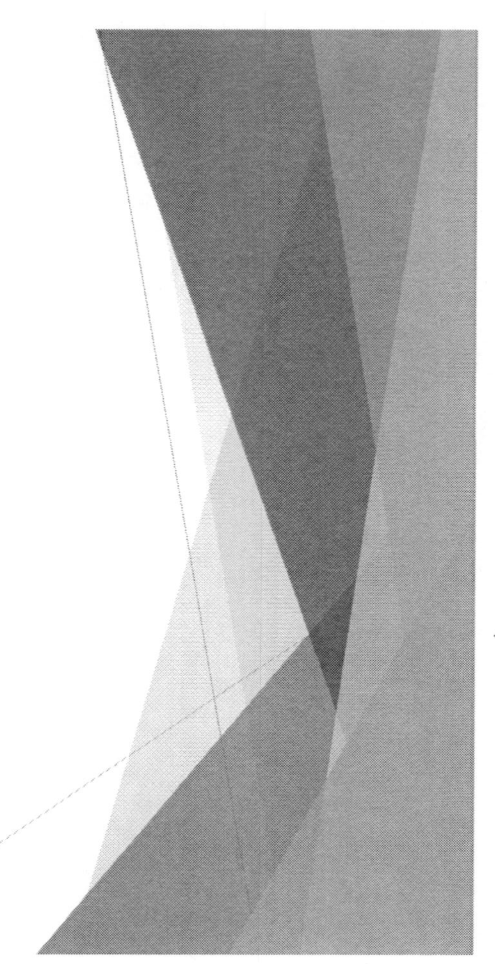

Similar to Caitra (Phillip Koehn) / CrossLang / TAUS DQF

iOmegaT (instrumented OmegaT)

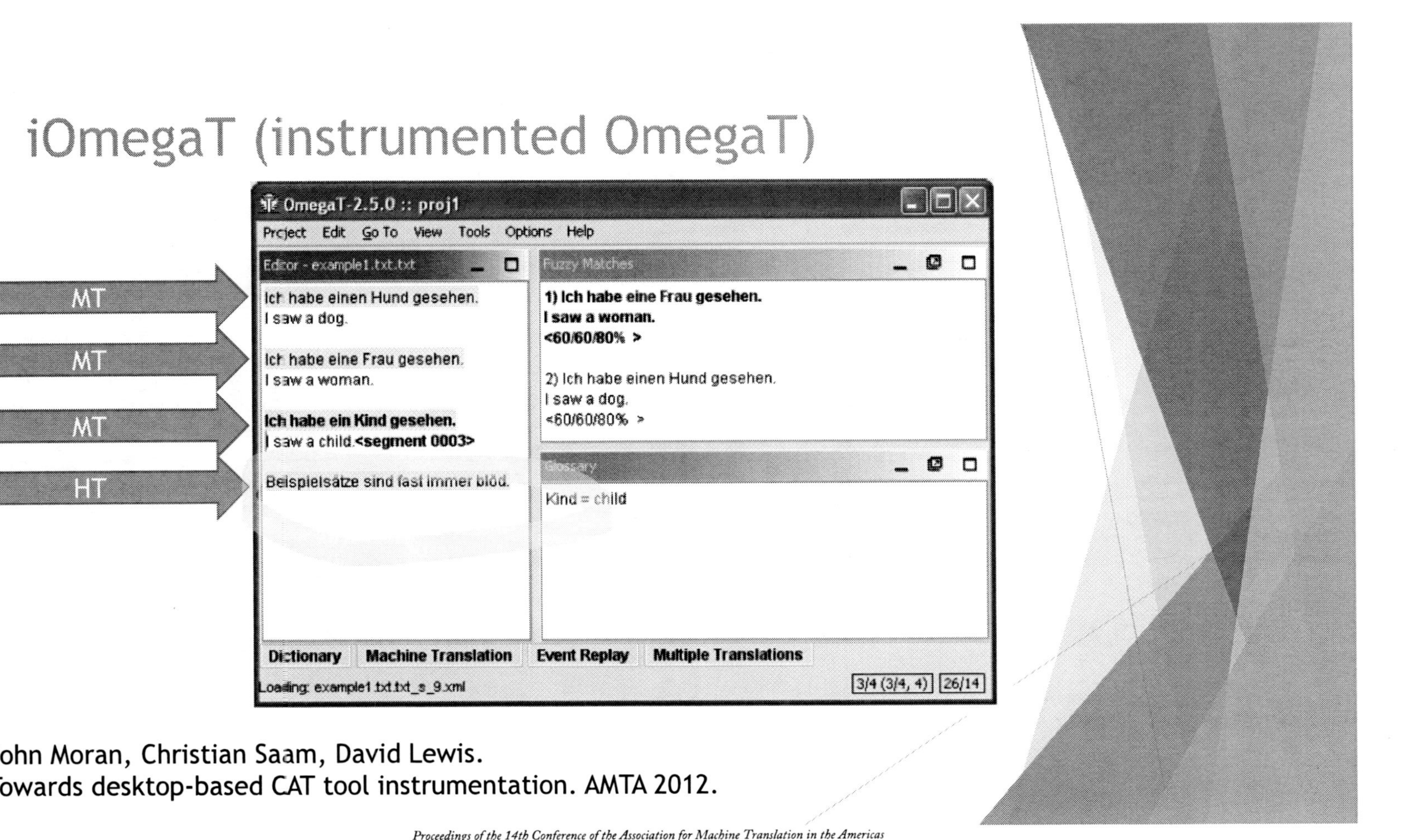

John Moran, Christian Saam, David Lewis.
Towards desktop-based CAT tool instrumentation. AMTA 2012.

fr_ca_tr1 – a rockstar posteditor, not identifiable using edit distance.

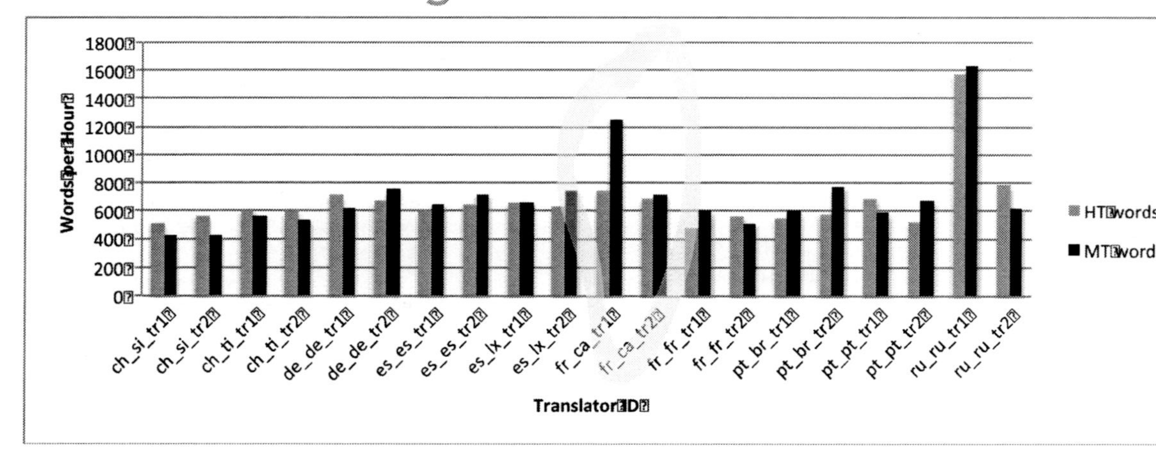

Thanks to Olga Beregovaya, Dave Clarke, Laura Casanellas @ Welocalize

Proceedings of the 14th Conference of the Association for Machine Translation in the Americas
October 6 – 9, 2020, 1st Workshop on Post-Editing in Modern-Day Translation

What we found

Rockstar (fast & good) post-editors exist but edit distance alone cannot help you find them as rockstar post-editors often make many edits fast.

MT saves time (but not always). It varies a lot between translators.

So, MT is as much a vendor management challenge as it is a technical one. Not every translator can (or should) post-edit.

(With exceptions) translators on the projects prefer to work in Trados than OmegaT.

IBM gathered very similar data over several months

"two studies demonstrate a significant increase in the productivity of human translators, on the order of about 50% in the first study and of 68% in the second study conducted a year later."

Salim Roukos, Abraham Ittycheriah, and Jian-Ming Xu. 2012. Document-specific statistical machine translation for improving human translation productivity. In Proceedings of the 13th international conference on Computational Linguistics and Intelligent Text Processing - Volume Part II, CICLing'12, pages 25–39, Berlin, Heidelberg. Springer-Verlag.

Proceedings of the 14th Conference of the Association for Machine Translation in the Americas
October 6 – 9, 2020, 1st Workshop on Post-Editing in Modern-Day Translation

Wordface Analytics

A plugin for Trados Studio – currently only used internally (and sporadically) in Transpiral

TAUS DQF (including Trados Plugin)

No HT baseline but MTPE speed gathered automatically

Proceedings of the 14th Conference of the Association for Machine Translation in the Americas
October 6 - 9, 2020, 1st Workshop on Post-Editing in Modern-Day Translation

MemoQ – Speed report

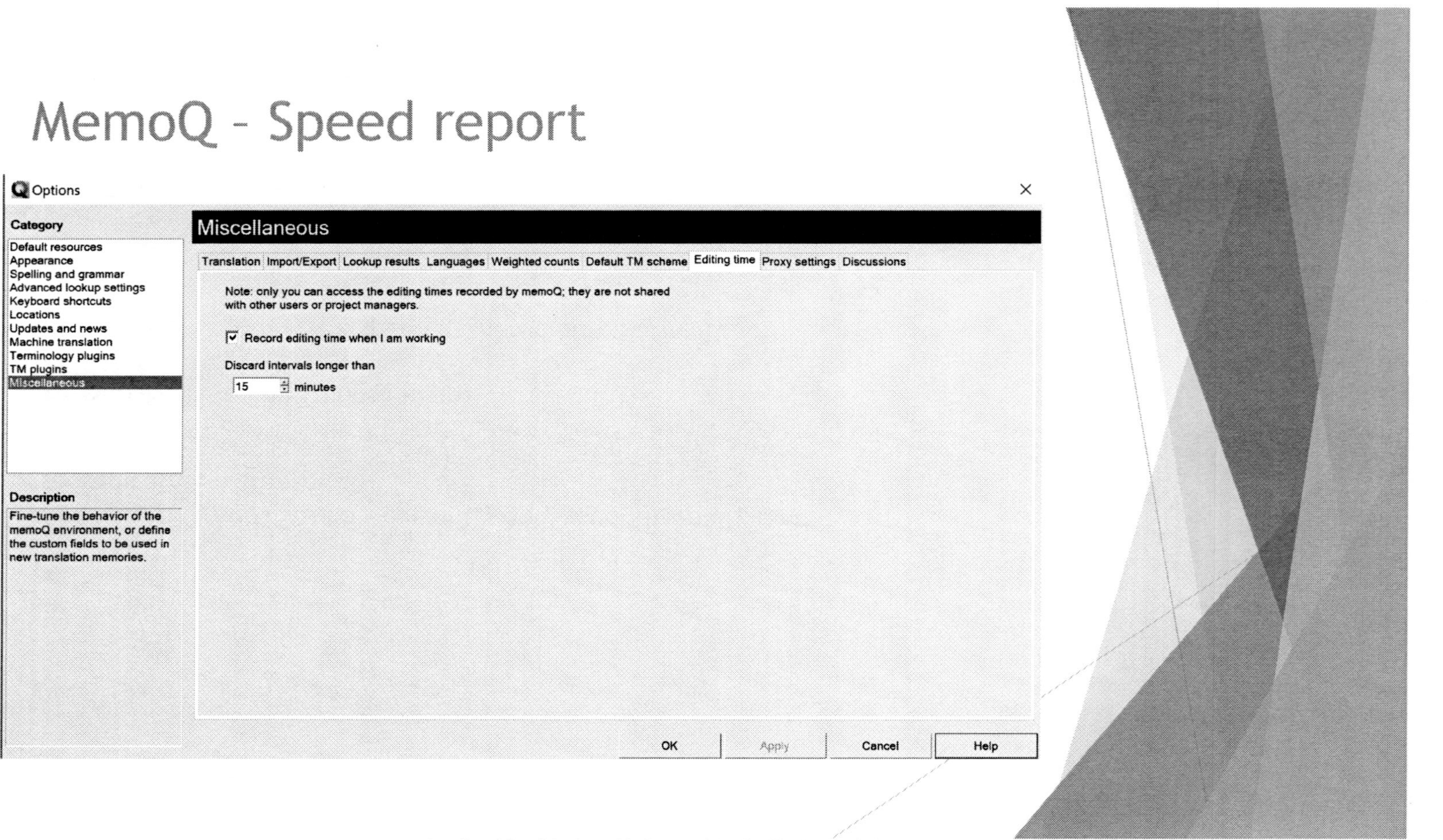

Proceedings of the 14th Conference of the Association for Machine Translation in the Americas
October 6 – 9, 2020, 1st Workshop on Post-Editing in Modern-Day Translation

MemoQ Speed Report

Type	Edit time	Words per hour
All	13,585	54324.62
X-Translated	0	0
101%	0	0
100%	01,027	94644.6
95%-99%	08,665	55256.78
85%-94%	0	0
75%-84%	0	0
50%-74%	0	0
Fragments	0	0
No match	03,893	41613.15

Note: not real data

Proceedings of the 14th Conference of the Association for Machine Translation in the Americas
October 6 - 9, 2020, 1st Workshop on Post-Editing in Modern-Day Translation

Web-based CAT tools

Typically free for translators

E.g. XTM, MemSource, WordBee, MateCAT and many more

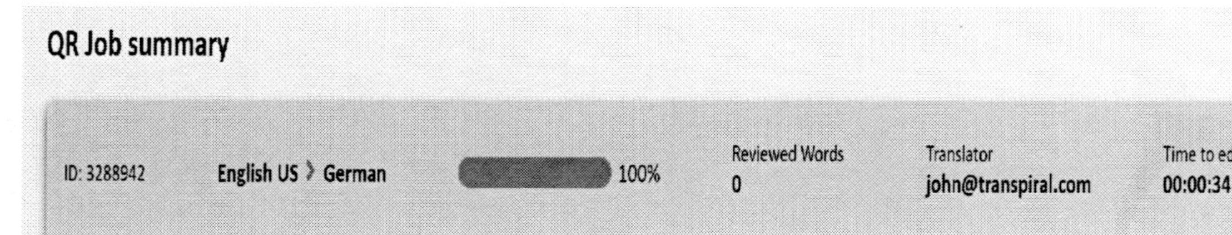

Screenshot from MateCAT: www.matecat.com

Proceedings of the 14th Conference of the Association for Machine Translation in the Americas
October 6 - 9, 2020, 1st Workshop on Post-Editing in Modern-Day Translation

An ideal commercial scenario

HT versus MT > MT versus MT

John Moran, Dave Lewis.
Unobtrusive methods for low-cost manual evaluation of machine translation, Tralogy 2011.

http://lodel.irevues.inist.fr/tralogy/index.php?id=141

The TMS or CAT tool helps the translator, LSP or buyer to choose the MT system

E.g. Lingua Custodia versus DeepL

or

Custom MT trained on Corpus A versus Corpus B

MemSource Translate

Quality Estimation and User Activity Data analysis to choose from 30 engines

Proceedings of the 14th Conference of the Association for Machine Translation in the Americas
October 6 - 9, 2020, 1st Workshop on Post-Editing in Modern-Day Translation

An ideal research scenario

Use an MT proxy pattern (e.g. via TMS, Intento, CrossLang) to test research systems in live translation projects

Measure post-hoc words per hour (or edit distance) perfomance in realtime

Switch to baseline if words per hour (or edit distance) declines too much

Publish automated metrics (BLEU, Meteor etc.) as well as PE performance data at AMTA

Proceedings of the 14th Conference of the Association for Machine Translation in the Americas
October 6 - 9, 2020, 1st Workshop on Post-Editing in Modern-Day Translation

Thank you for listening!

john@transpiral.com

https://www.linkedin.com/in/johndesmondmoran/

Proceedings of the 14th Conference of the Association for Machine Translation in the Americas
October 6 – 9, 2020, 1st Workshop on Post-Editing in Modern-Day Translation

Help Me! Those Free and/or Open Source Machine Translation Tools!

- An Small Exploratory Experiment with EN<>FR, EN<>ES and EN<>ZH translation

Presented by:
Serene Su

**at the AMTA 2020 | 1st Workshop on Post-Editing in Modern-Day Translation
On October 6, 2020**

Disclaimer

n exploratory experiment

- Background
- Limitations
- Caveats

An exploratory experiment

- 5 popular free and/or open source machine translation tools
- Two contexts: legal and medical; public info
- English<>French, English<>Spanish & English<>Chinese
- review their performances in terms of BLEU scores with comparison to human translation

Translation Task One (Legal): *The Grand Jury ~ 316 words*

Source: https://www.nycourts.gov/litigants/crimjusticesyshandbk.shtml#anchor751950

Grand jury proceedings are secret and are not open to the public. The grand jury is made up of sixteen to twenty-three people who listen to the evidence and decide whether there is enough evidence to put you on trial for a felony. If the grand jurors decide that there is enough evidence, they vote an indictment.

You have the right to testify before the grand jury. Although your lawyer may go with you to the proceeding, he or she must remain silent during your testimony. Your lawyer may not address the grand jury or object to the prosecutor's questions. If you want to speak with your lawyer before testifying, you may do so outside the grand jury room. Any conversation you have with your lawyer inside the grand jury room must be whispered and must not be heard by the grand jurors.

If you decide to testify before the grand jury, you will probably be cross-examined by the prosecutor. Any questions the grand jurors may have for you will be asked by the prosecutor.

You may also ask that the grand jury hear witnesses willing to testify for you, although you are not allowed to be present in the grand jury room while they testify.

If the grand jury does not vote an indictment, you will be released from jail. If the grand jury votes an indictment, your case will be transferred from Criminal Court to Supreme Court for another arraignment within a few weeks. This arraignment is similar to the arraignment in Criminal Court. You will be formally charged with the crime(s) voted by the grand jury and contained in the indictment, and you will plead either guilty or not guilty. The conditions of your bail may also be reviewed and plea bargaining may take place. If you do not plead guilty, your case will be adjourned to a calendar part.

Translation Task Two (Medical): *Anaphylaxis~ 272 words*

source: https://healthtranslations.vic.gov.au/bhcv2/bhcht.nsf/PresentDetail?Open&s=Anaphylaxis

Anaphylaxis i[s] potentially life threatening, severe allergic reaction and should always be treated as a medical emergency. Anaphylaxis occurs after exposure to an allergen (usually to foods, insects or medicines), to which a person is allergic. Not all people with allergies are at risk of anaphylaxis.
It is important to know the signs and symptoms of anaphylaxis. Symptoms of anaphylaxis are potentially life threatening and include any one of the following:
• Difficult/noisy breathing.
• Swelling of the tongue.
• Swelling/tightness in the throat.
• Difficulty talking and/or hoarse voice.
• Wheeze or persistent cough.
• Persistent dizziness and/or collapse.
• Pale and floppy (in young children).
In some cases, anaphylaxis is preceded by less dangerous allergic symptoms such as:
• Swelling of face, lips and/or eyes.
• Hives or welts.
• Abdominal pain and vomiting (these are signs of anaphylaxis for insect allergy).
Several factors can influence the severity of an allergic reaction. These include exercise, heat, alcohol, and in food allergic people; the amount of food eaten and how it is prepared.
Identifying the cause of anaphylaxis is important.
Your doctor will normally ask a series of questions that may help to narrow down the list of likely causes such as foods or medicines consumed that day, or exposure to insects. This approach will also help to exclude conditions that can sometimes be confused with anaphylaxis, such as fainting or an epileptic seizure. If allergy is suspected, this may be followed by allergy tests, usually a blood test for allergen specific IgE (formerly known as RAST tests) or skin prick testing, to help confirm or exclude potential triggers.

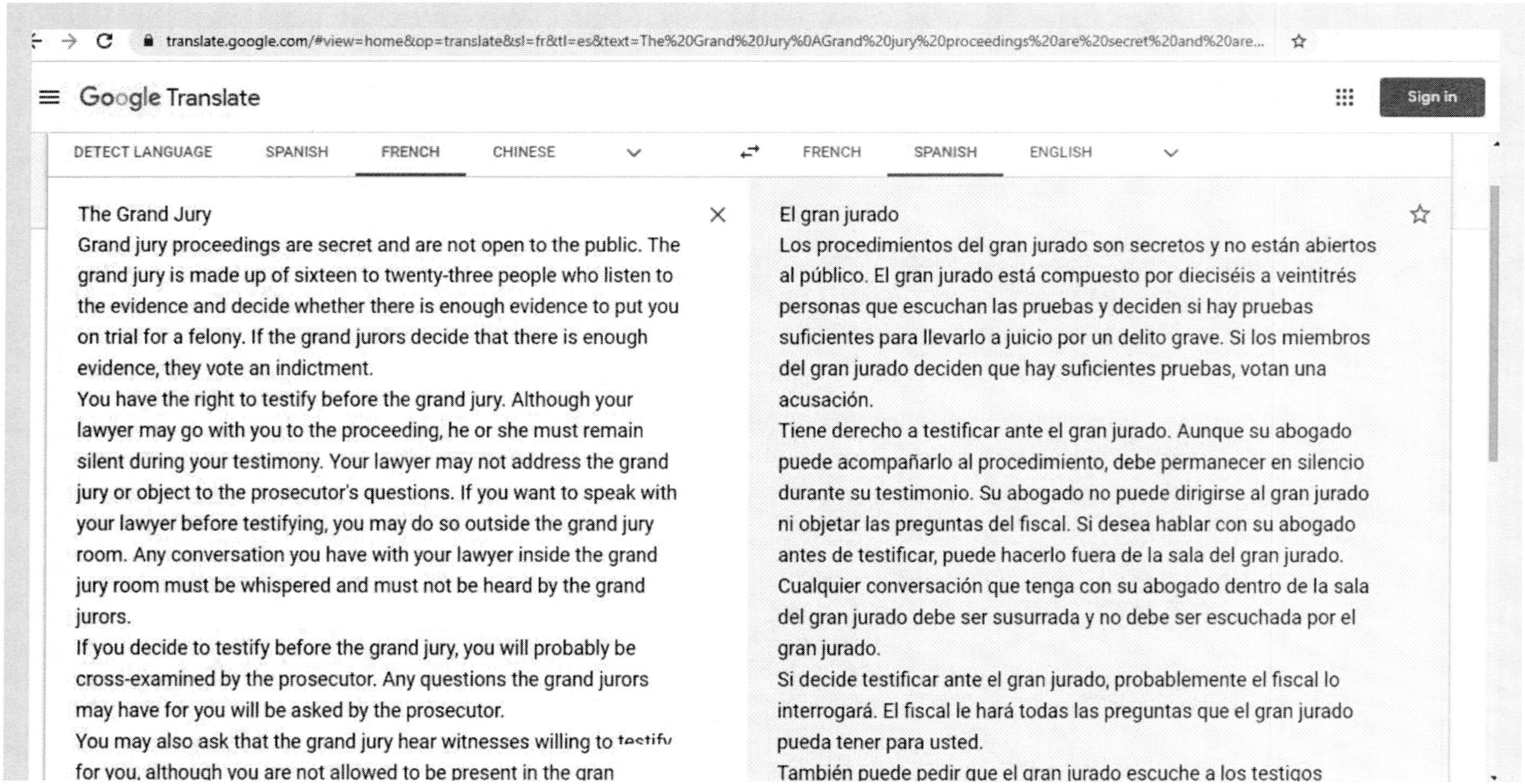

translate.google.com/#view=home&op=translate&sl=fr&tl=es&text=The%20Grand%20Jury%0AGrand%20jury%20proceedings%20are%20secret%20and%20are...

Google Translate

Sign in

| DETECT LANGUAGE | SPANISH | FRENCH | CHINESE | | | FRENCH | SPANISH | ENGLISH |

The Grand Jury

Grand jury proceedings are secret and are not open to the public. The grand jury is made up of sixteen to twenty-three people who listen to the evidence and decide whether there is enough evidence to put you on trial for a felony. If the grand jurors decide that there is enough evidence, they vote an indictment.

You have the right to testify before the grand jury. Although your lawyer may go with you to the proceeding, he or she must remain silent during your testimony. Your lawyer may not address the grand jury or object to the prosecutor's questions. If you want to speak with your lawyer before testifying, you may do so outside the grand jury room. Any conversation you have with your lawyer inside the grand jury room must be whispered and must not be heard by the grand jurors.

If you decide to testify before the grand jury, you will probably be cross-examined by the prosecutor. Any questions the grand jurors may have for you will be asked by the prosecutor.

You may also ask that the grand jury hear witnesses willing to testify for you, although you are not allowed to be present in the gran

El gran jurado

Los procedimientos del gran jurado son secretos y no están abiertos al público. El gran jurado está compuesto por dieciséis a veintitrés personas que escuchan las pruebas y deciden si hay pruebas suficientes para llevarlo a juicio por un delito grave. Si los miembros del gran jurado deciden que hay suficientes pruebas, votan una acusación.

Tiene derecho a testificar ante el gran jurado. Aunque su abogado puede acompañarlo al procedimiento, debe permanecer en silencio durante su testimonio. Su abogado no puede dirigirse al gran jurado ni objetar las preguntas del fiscal. Si desea hablar con su abogado antes de testificar, puede hacerlo fuera de la sala del gran jurado. Cualquier conversación que tenga con su abogado dentro de la sala del gran jurado debe ser susurrada y no debe ser escuchada por el gran jurado.

Si decide testificar ante el gran jurado, probablemente el fiscal lo interrogará. El fiscal le hará todas las preguntas que el gran jurado pueda tener para usted.

También puede pedir que el gran jurado escuche a los testigos

translate.systran.net/translationTools/text?source=en&target=es&input=The+Grand+Jury%0D%0AGrand+jury+proceedings+are+secret+and+are+not+open+to...

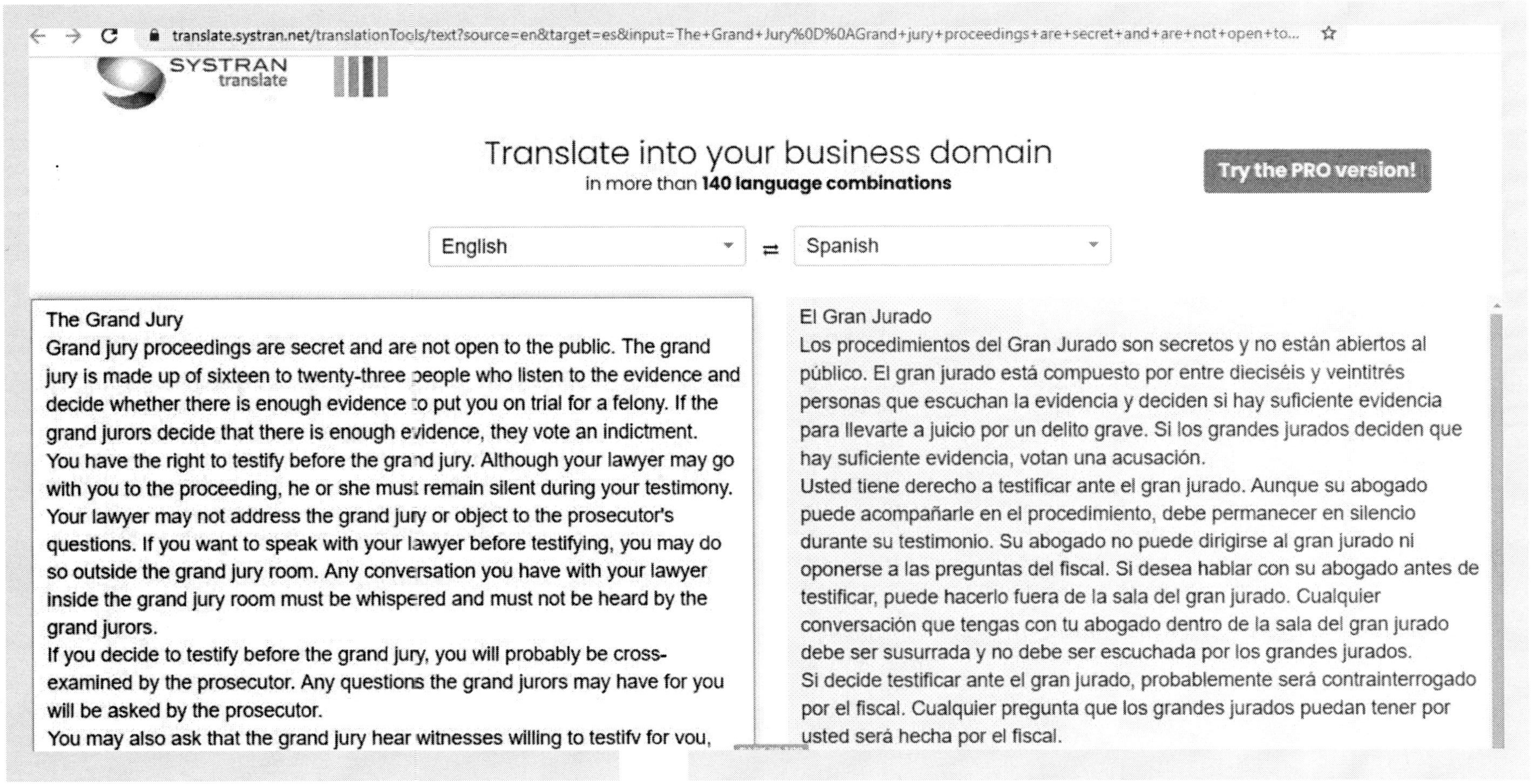

SYSTRAN
translate

Translate into your business domain
in more than 140 language combinations

Try the PRO version!

English ⇄ Spanish

The Grand Jury
Grand jury proceedings are secret and are not open to the public. The grand jury is made up of sixteen to twenty-three people who listen to the evidence and decide whether there is enough evidence to put you on trial for a felony. If the grand jurors decide that there is enough evidence, they vote an indictment.
You have the right to testify before the grand jury. Although your lawyer may go with you to the proceeding, he or she must remain silent during your testimony. Your lawyer may not address the grand jury or object to the prosecutor's questions. If you want to speak with your lawyer before testifying, you may do so outside the grand jury room. Any conversation you have with your lawyer inside the grand jury room must be whispered and must not be heard by the grand jurors.
If you decide to testify before the grand jury, you will probably be cross-examined by the prosecutor. Any questions the grand jurors may have for you will be asked by the prosecutor.
You may also ask that the grand jury hear witnesses willing to testify for you,

El Gran Jurado
Los procedimientos del Gran Jurado son secretos y no están abiertos al público. El gran jurado está compuesto por entre dieciséis y veintitrés personas que escuchan la evidencia y deciden si hay suficiente evidencia para llevarte a juicio por un delito grave. Si los grandes jurados deciden que hay suficiente evidencia, votan una acusación.
Usted tiene derecho a testificar ante el gran jurado. Aunque su abogado puede acompañarle en el procedimiento, debe permanecer en silencio durante su testimonio. Su abogado no puede dirigirse al gran jurado ni oponerse a las preguntas del fiscal. Si desea hablar con su abogado antes de testificar, puede hacerlo fuera de la sala del gran jurado. Cualquier conversación que tengas con tu abogado dentro de la sala del gran jurado debe ser susurrada y no debe ser escuchada por los grandes jurados.
Si decide testificar ante el gran jurado, probablemente será contrainterrogado por el fiscal. Cualquier pregunta que los grandes jurados puedan tener por usted será hecha por el fiscal.

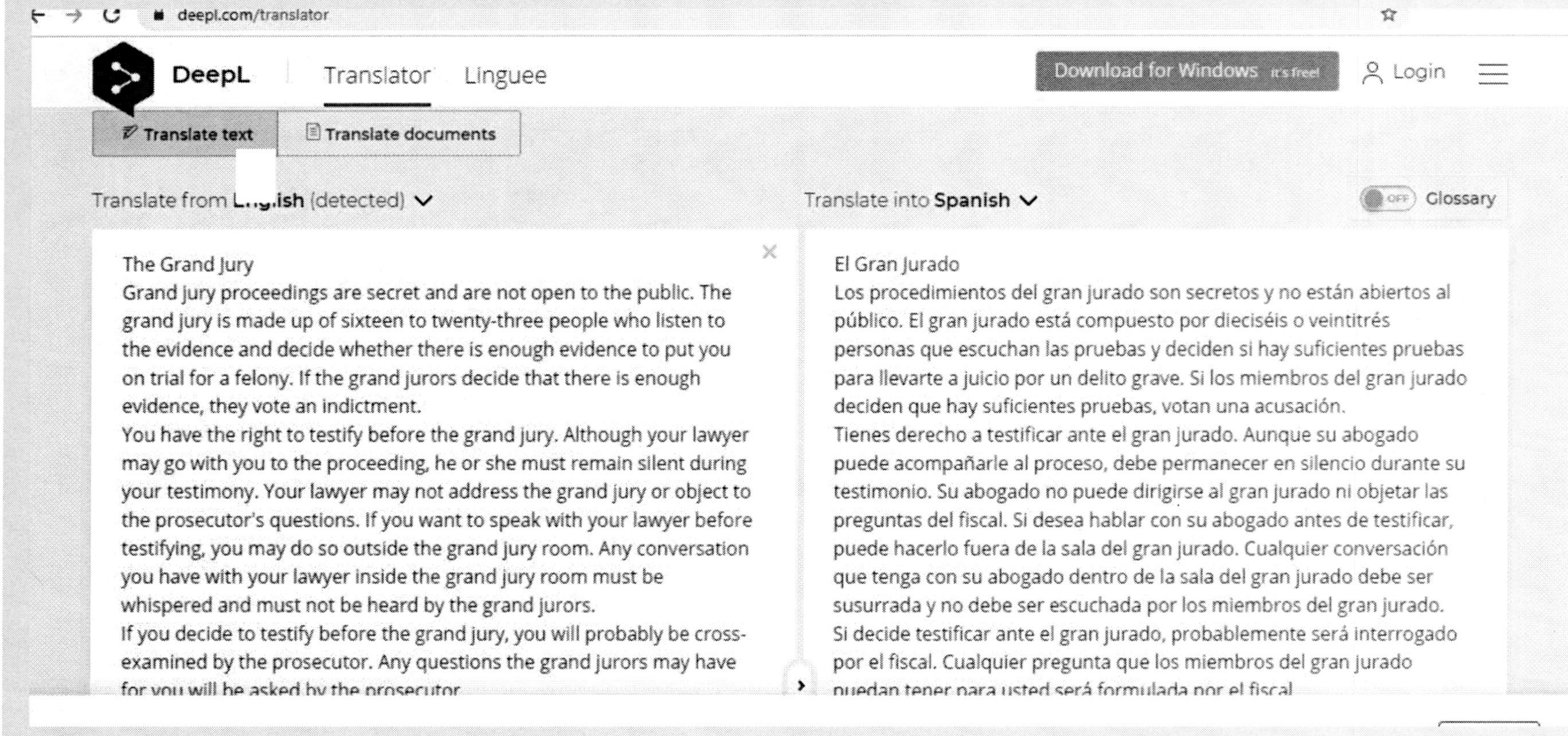
deepl.com/translator
DeepL   Translator   Linguee
Download for Windows   It's free!
Login
Translate text   Translate documents
Translate from English (detected)
Translate into Spanish
Glossary

The Grand Jury
Grand jury proceedings are secret and are not open to the public. The grand jury is made up of sixteen to twenty-three people who listen to the evidence and decide whether there is enough evidence to put you on trial for a felony. If the grand jurors decide that there is enough evidence, they vote an indictment.
You have the right to testify before the grand jury. Although your lawyer may go with you to the proceeding, he or she must remain silent during your testimony. Your lawyer may not address the grand jury or object to the prosecutor's questions. If you want to speak with your lawyer before testifying, you may do so outside the grand jury room. Any conversation you have with your lawyer inside the grand jury room must be whispered and must not be heard by the grand jurors.
If you decide to testify before the grand jury, you will probably be cross-examined by the prosecutor. Any questions the grand jurors may have for you will be asked by the prosecutor

El Gran Jurado
Los procedimientos del gran jurado son secretos y no están abiertos al público. El gran jurado está compuesto por dieciséis o veintitrés personas que escuchan las pruebas y deciden si hay suficientes pruebas para llevarte a juicio por un delito grave. Si los miembros del gran jurado deciden que hay suficientes pruebas, votan una acusación.
Tienes derecho a testificar ante el gran jurado. Aunque su abogado puede acompañarle al proceso, debe permanecer en silencio durante su testimonio. Su abogado no puede dirigirse al gran jurado ni objetar las preguntas del fiscal. Si desea hablar con su abogado antes de testificar, puede hacerlo fuera de la sala del gran jurado. Cualquier conversación que tenga con su abogado dentro de la sala del gran jurado debe ser susurrada y no debe ser escuchada por los miembros del gran jurado.
Si decide testificar ante el gran jurado, probablemente será interrogado por el fiscal. Cualquier pregunta que los miembros del gran jurado puedan tener para usted será formulada por el fiscal

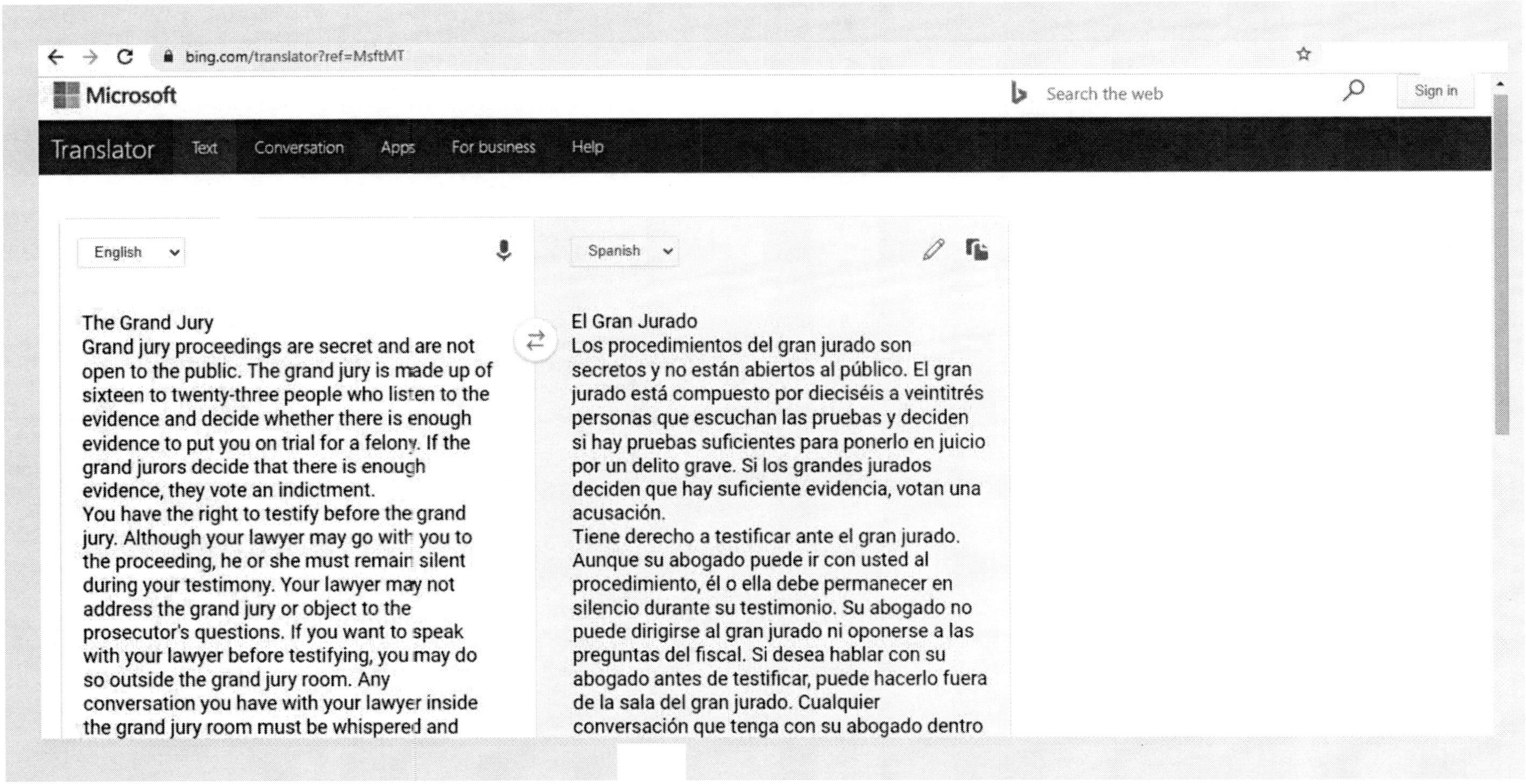

bing.com/translator?ref=MsftMT

Microsoft

Search the web

Sign in

Translator   Text   Conversation   Apps   For business   Help

English   Spanish

The Grand Jury
Grand jury proceedings are secret and are not open to the public. The grand jury is made up of sixteen to twenty-three people who listen to the evidence and decide whether there is enough evidence to put you on trial for a felony. If the grand jurors decide that there is enough evidence, they vote an indictment.
You have the right to testify before the grand jury. Although your lawyer may go with you to the proceeding, he or she must remain silent during your testimony. Your lawyer may not address the grand jury or object to the prosecutor's questions. If you want to speak with your lawyer before testifying, you may do so outside the grand jury room. Any conversation you have with your lawyer inside the grand jury room must be whispered and

El Gran Jurado
Los procedimientos del gran jurado son secretos y no están abiertos al público. El gran jurado está compuesto por dieciséis a veintitrés personas que escuchan las pruebas y deciden si hay pruebas suficientes para ponerlo en juicio por un delito grave. Si los grandes jurados deciden que hay suficiente evidencia, votan una acusación.
Tiene derecho a testificar ante el gran jurado. Aunque su abogado puede ir con usted al procedimiento, él o ella debe permanecer en silencio durante su testimonio. Su abogado no puede dirigirse al gran jurado ni oponerse a las preguntas del fiscal. Si desea hablar con su abogado antes de testificar, puede hacerlo fuera de la sala del gran jurado. Cualquier conversación que tenga con su abogado dentro

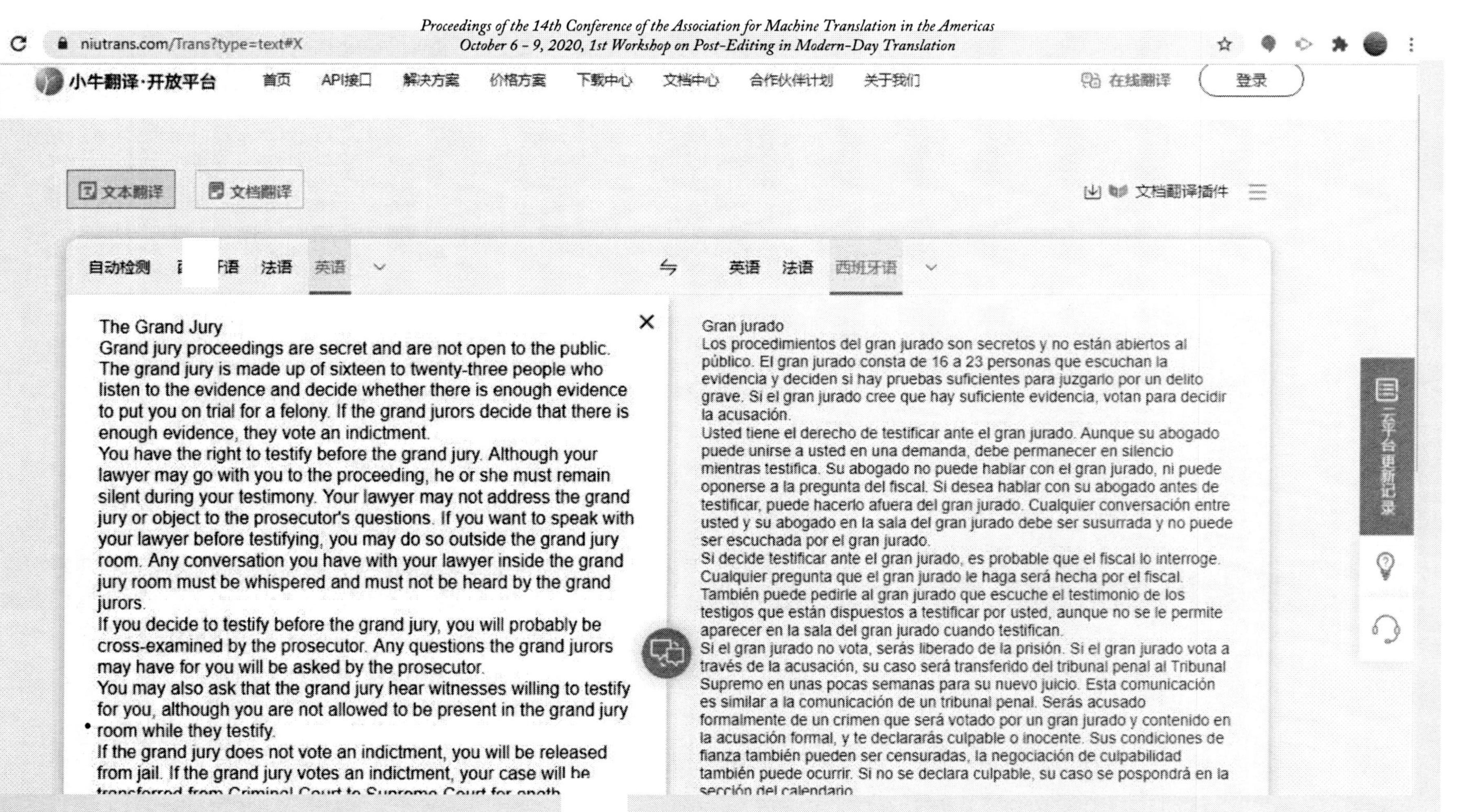
niutrans.com/Trans?type=text#X
小牛翻译·开放平台
首页　API接口　解决方案　价格方案　下载中心　文档中心　合作伙伴计划　关于我们
在线翻译
登录
文本翻译
文档翻译
文档翻译插件
自动检测　英语　法语　英语　⇆　英语　法语　西班牙语
二石平台更新记录

The Grand Jury
Grand jury proceedings are secret and are not open to the public.
The grand jury is made up of sixteen to twenty-three people who
listen to the evidence and decide whether there is enough evidence
to put you on trial for a felony. If the grand jurors decide that there is
enough evidence, they vote an indictment.
You have the right to testify before the grand jury. Although your
lawyer may go with you to the proceeding, he or she must remain
silent during your testimony. Your lawyer may not address the grand
jury or object to the prosecutor's questions. If you want to speak with
your lawyer before testifying, you may do so outside the grand jury
room. Any conversation you have with your lawyer inside the grand
jury room must be whispered and must not be heard by the grand
jurors.
If you decide to testify before the grand jury, you will probably be
cross-examined by the prosecutor. Any questions the grand jurors
may have for you will be asked by the prosecutor.
You may also ask that the grand jury hear witnesses willing to testify
for you, although you are not allowed to be present in the grand jury
room while they testify.
If the grand jury does not vote an indictment, you will be released
from jail. If the grand jury votes an indictment, your case will be
transferred from Criminal Court to Supreme Court for anoth

Gran jurado
Los procedimientos del gran jurado son secretos y no están abiertos al
público. El gran jurado consta de 16 a 23 personas que escuchan la
evidencia y deciden si hay pruebas suficientes para juzgarlo por un delito
grave. Si el gran jurado cree que hay suficiente evidencia, votan para decidir
la acusación.
Usted tiene el derecho de testificar ante el gran jurado. Aunque su abogado
puede unirse a usted en una demanda, debe permanecer en silencio
mientras testifica. Su abogado no puede hablar con el gran jurado, ni puede
oponerse a la pregunta del fiscal. Si desea hablar con su abogado antes de
testificar, puede hacerlo afuera del gran jurado. Cualquier conversación entre
usted y su abogado en la sala del gran jurado debe ser susurrada y no puede
ser escuchada por el gran jurado.
Si decide testificar ante el gran jurado, es probable que el fiscal lo interrogue.
Cualquier pregunta que el gran jurado le haga será hecha por el fiscal.
También puede pedirle al gran jurado que escuche el testimonio de los
testigos que están dispuestos a testificar por usted, aunque no se le permite
aparecer en la sala del gran jurado cuando testifican.
Si el gran jurado no vota, serás liberado de la prisión. Si el gran jurado vota a
través de la acusación, su caso será transferido del tribunal penal al Tribunal
Supremo en unas pocas semanas para su nuevo juicio. Esta comunicación
es similar a la comunicación de un tribunal penal. Serás acusado
formalmente de un crimen que será votado por un gran jurado y contenido en
la acusación formal, y te declararás culpable o inocente. Sus condiciones de
fianza también pueden ser censuradas, la negociación de culpabilidad
también puede ocurrir. Si no se declara culpable, su caso se pospondrá en la
sección del calendario

Evaluation Methods and BLEU score:

- Measures how many words overlap when comparing a raw MT output Vs. a human "golden" reference translation

- More overlap, higher the score

- Broadly speaking, scores of
  - 30 ~ 50: could be of some help
  - 50 ~ 59: good for use with some PE
  - 60~ 69: mostly accurate & fluent
  - 70+: ?

Translation Task One (Legal): *The Grand Jury ~ 316 words*

BLEU Scores Comparison

GrandJury	Google Translate	Systran	DeepL	Microsoft Bing	NiuTrans
EN>ES	35.69	8.51	35.38	35.49	10.43
ES>EN	42.44	9.02	38.11	30.51	13.47
EN>FR	12.83	11.16	11.06	12.35	8.21
FR>EN	21.1	17.85	21.38	21.88	16.34
EN>ZH	3.72	3.42	1.81	1.94	3.68
ZH>EN	24.72	25.22	26.43	25.72	36.41

Proceedings of the 14th Conference of the Association for Machine Translation in the Americas
October 6 – 9, 2020, 1st Workshop on Post-Editing in Modern-Day Translation

Translation Task Two (Medical): _Anaphylaxis~ 272 words_

BLEU Scores Comparison

Anaphylaxis	Google Translate	Systran	DeepL	Microsoft Bing	NiuTrans
EN>ES	42.49	37.44	40.08	43.94	25.58
ES>EN	47.65	53.88	48.49	43.41	26.33
EN>FR	23.88	17.26	18.18	27.98	18.02
FR>EN	23.17	24.59	24.45	24.17	15.56
EN>ZH	3.73	3.4	1.18	1.29	1.21
ZH>EN	24.7	23.78	35.81	24.81	12.07

Findings

Translation Task One (Legal): *The Grand Jury ~ 316 words*

BLEU Scores Comparison

GrandJury	Google Translate	Systran	DeepL	Microsoft Bing	NiuTrans
EN>ES	35.69	8.51	35.38	35.49	10.43
ES>EN	42.44	9.02	38.11	30.51	13.47
EN>FR	12.83	11.16	11.06	12.35	8.21
FR>EN	21.1	17.85	21.38	21.88	16.34
EN>ZH	3.72	3.42	1.81	1.94	3.68
ZH>EN	24.72	25.22	26.43	25.72	36.41

Translation Task Two (Medical): _Anaphylaxis~ 272 words_

BLEU Scores Comparison

Anaphylaxis	Google Translate	Systran	DeepL	Microsoft Bing	NiuTrans
EN>ES	42.49	37.44	40.08	43.94	25.58
ES>EN	47.65	53.88	48.49	43.41	26.33
EN>FR	23.88	17.26	18.18	27.98	18.02
FR>EN	23.17	24.59	24.45	24.17	15.56
EN>ZH	3.73	3.4	1.18	1.29	1.21
ZH>EN	24.7	23.78	35.81	24.81	12.07

Proceedings of the 14th Conference of the Association for Machine Translation in the Americas
October 6 – 9, 2020, 1st Workshop on Post-Editing in Modern-Day Translation

Ti_ne spent:

Human only: 1-2 hrs
Vs.
PEMT: 15-30 mins

Translation Task Two (Medical): Anaphylaxis~ 272 wo

BLEU Scores Comparison

Anaphylaxis	Google Translate	Systran	DeepL	Microsoft Bing	NiuTrans
EN>ES	42.49	37.44	40.08	43.94	25.58
ES>EN	47.65	53.88	48.49	43.41	26.33
EN>FR	23.88	17.26	18.18	27.98	18.02
FR>EN	23.17	24.59	24.45	24.17	15.56
EN>ZH	3.73	3.4	1.18	1.29	1.21
ZH>EN	24.7	23.78	35.81	24.81	12.07

Translation Task Two (Medical): _Anaphylaxis~ 272 wo..._

BLEU Scores Comparison

Anaphylaxis	Google Translate	Systran	DeepL	Microsoft Bing	NiuTrans
EN>ES	42.49	37.44	40.08	43.94	25.58
ES>EN	47.65	53.88	48.49	43.41	26.33
EN>FR	23.88	17.26	18.18	27.98	18.02
FR>EN	23.17	24.59	24.45	24.17	15.56
EN>ZH	3.73	3.4	1.18	1.29	1.21
ZH>EN	24.7	23.78	35.81	24.81	12.07

An exploratory experiment - Findings and Suggestions

- Language combinations:
  - EN<>ES generally better than EN<>FR
  - both EN<>ES and EN<>FR generally better than EN<>ZH based on this experiment, with a few exceptions
- Certain MT performs better in certain language combinations based on this experiment
- The availability of all the Interet info related to subject matters in multiple languages
- Get basic meaning in time-sensitive situations
- Race with machine…save time and gain productivity in certain scenarios
- Reference point and possibly to further experiment for working translators, interpreters, LSPs and machine translation developers
- Controversy…

As ⁻lways, feedback is welcome:
serenesou666@gmail.com

With thanks (for examples, testing and discussions):
Evelyn G; Jingyi W; Lucy L; Anna C; River L; Maria J; Lenny Y;
Michael W and Matt G

LANG.TEC

SEMANTIC TEXT PROCESSING

Proceedings of the 14th Conference of the Association for Machine Translation in the Americas
October 6 - 9, 20:   rkshop on Post-Editing in Modern-Day Translation

LANG.TEC

SEMANTIC TEXT PROCESSING

Proceedings of the 14th Conference of the Association for Machine Translation in the Americas
October 6 - 9, 20.   rkshop on Post-Editing in Modern-Day Translation

Presentation Outline

LANG.TEC

SEMANTIC TEXT PROCESSING

1. Who we are
2. Business areas
3. Clients
4. Introducing QUEST – the MT Quality Estimator
5. Comparing translation modes (HT, PEMT, QUEST)
6. Demo
7. Model architecture
8. Parting words

Proceedings of the 14th Conference of the Association for Machine Translation in the Americas
October 6 – 9, 20:   rkshop on Post–Editing in Modern–Day Translation

Who we are

LANG.TEC

SEMANTIC TEXT PROCESSING

LangTec:

- 10 years in business, 15 employees
  We've been working on MTQE since 2018
- QUEST is our second fully functioning QE model and a significant advance over its predecessor

Proceedings of the 14th Conference of the Association for Machine Translation in the Americas
October 6 - 9, 20.   rkshop on Post-Editing in Modern-Day Translation

Business areas

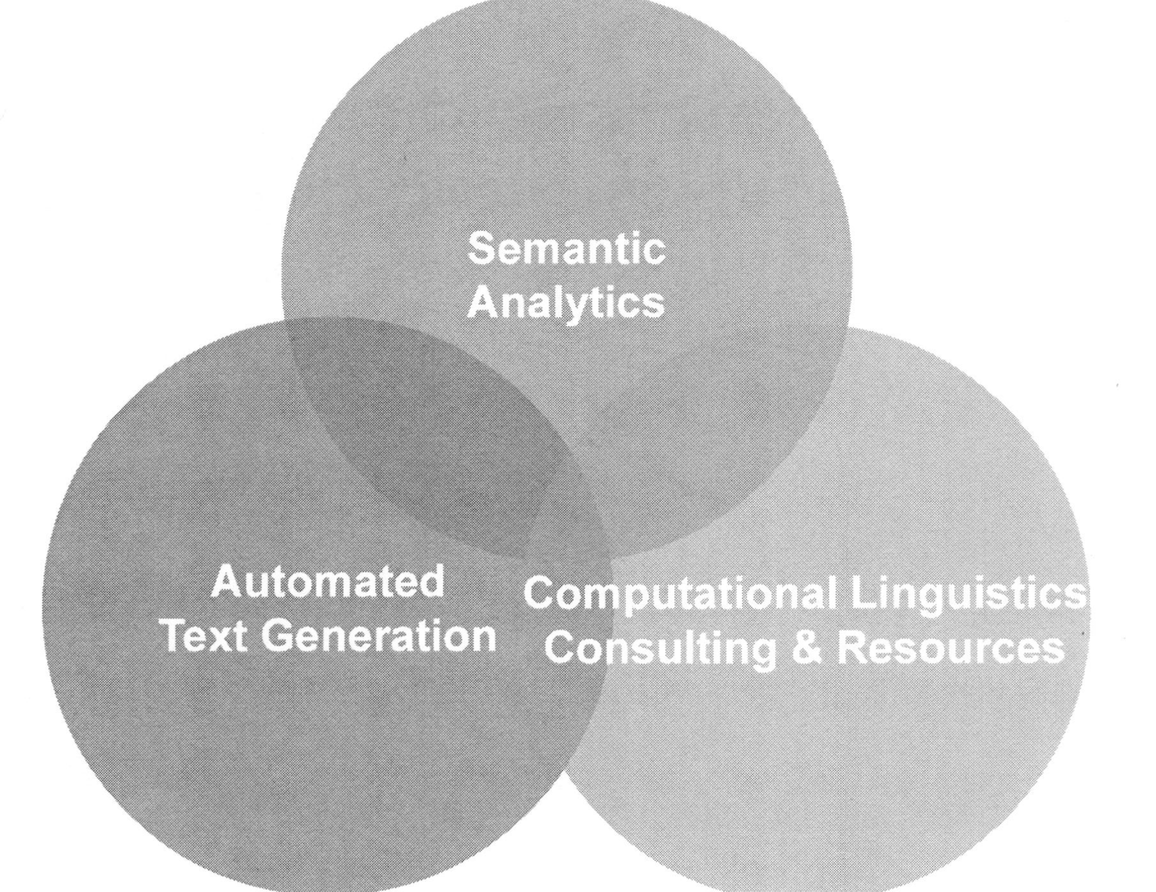

Proceedings of the 14th Conference of the Association for Machine Translation in the Americas
October 6 - 9, 20:   rkshop on Post-Editing in Modern-Day Translation

Clients

1. Semantic Analytics

Clients

2. Automated Text Generation

Proceedings of the 14th Conference of the Association for Machine Translation in the Americas
October 6 – 9, 20:   rkshop on Post-Editing in Modern-Day Translation

Clients

3. Computational Linguistics

SEMANTIC TEXT PROCESSING

Proceedings of the 14th Conference of the Association for Machine Translation in the Americas
October 6 – 9, 20·   rkshop on Post-Editing in Modern-Day Translation

Introducing QUEST –
MT Quality Estimator

Proceedings of the 14th Conference of the Association for Machine Translation in the Americas
October 6 - 9, 20:   rkshop on Post-Editing in Modern-Day Translation

Overview

1. Our in-domain QUEST model is capable of predicting post-editing effort with unprecedented accuracy: only 2% error

2. QUEST can be used with any language pair, any machine translation engine and for any domain.

3. QUEST can also be used out-of-domain still providing superior prediction accuracy compared with experience-based estimations and other machine learning models

4. QUEST's prediction accuracy enables translation service providers to achieve much more competitive pricing and deadline-setting.

Proceedings of the 14th Conference of the Association for Machine Translation in the Americas
October 6 - 9, 20:   rkshop on Post-Editing in Modern-Day Translation

In-Domain QUEST Model

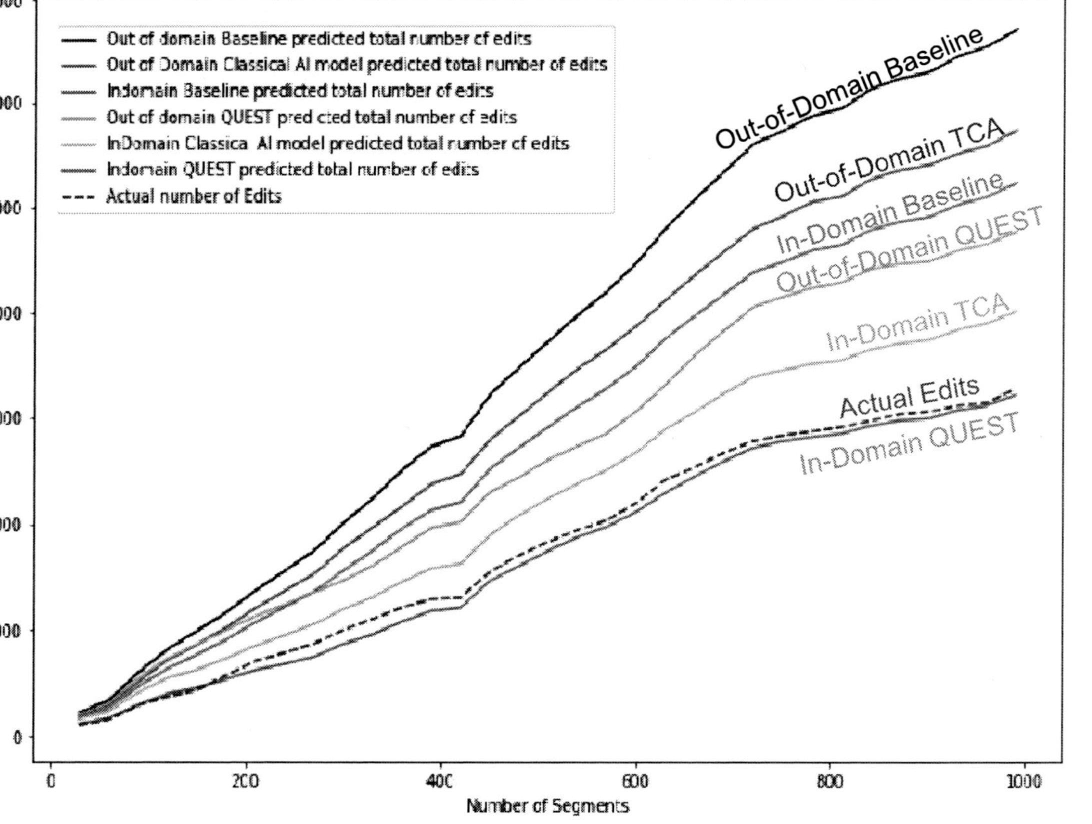

- When historical domain data are available we can also train in-domain models.

- The in-domain baseline beats the out-of-domain baseline.

- The in-domain baseline also beats the out-of-domain TCA.

- The out-of-domain QUEST model beats all baselines and the out-of-domain TCA.

- The in-domain QUEST model beats all baselines and all TCA models, very closely approximating the actual post-editing effort.

Proceedings of the 14th Conference of the Association for Machine Translation in the Americas
October 6 – 9, 20:   rkshop on Post-Editing in Modern-Day Translation

Comparing approaches

	Manual Translation (HT)	MT + Post-Editing (In-domain baseline)	MT + Post-Editing + QUEST (out-of-domain)	MT + post-editing + QUEST (in-domain)	Actual
Word Count	22,635	22,635	22,635	22,635	22,635
Predicted Post-Editing Opera ns	0	10,474	9,538	**6,443**	6,561
Prediction Error	0%	60%	45%	**2%**	0%
Total Turnover Effort	56.59 hrs. 7.07 person days	48.00 hrs. 6.00 person days	43.72 person hrs. 5.46 person days	**29.53 hrs. 3.69 person days**	30.07 hrs 3.76 person days
Fraction of words to be processed	100%	46%	42%	**28%**	29%
Per-Word Rate	EUR 0.09	EUR 0.05	EUR 0.04	**EUR 0.03**	EUR 0.03
Total Cost	EUR 2,037	EUR 1,132	EUR 905	**EUR 679**	EUR 679

Proceedings of the 14th Conference of the Association for Machine Translation in the Americas
October 6 – 9, 20:   rkshop on Post–Editing in Modern–Day Translation

Demo

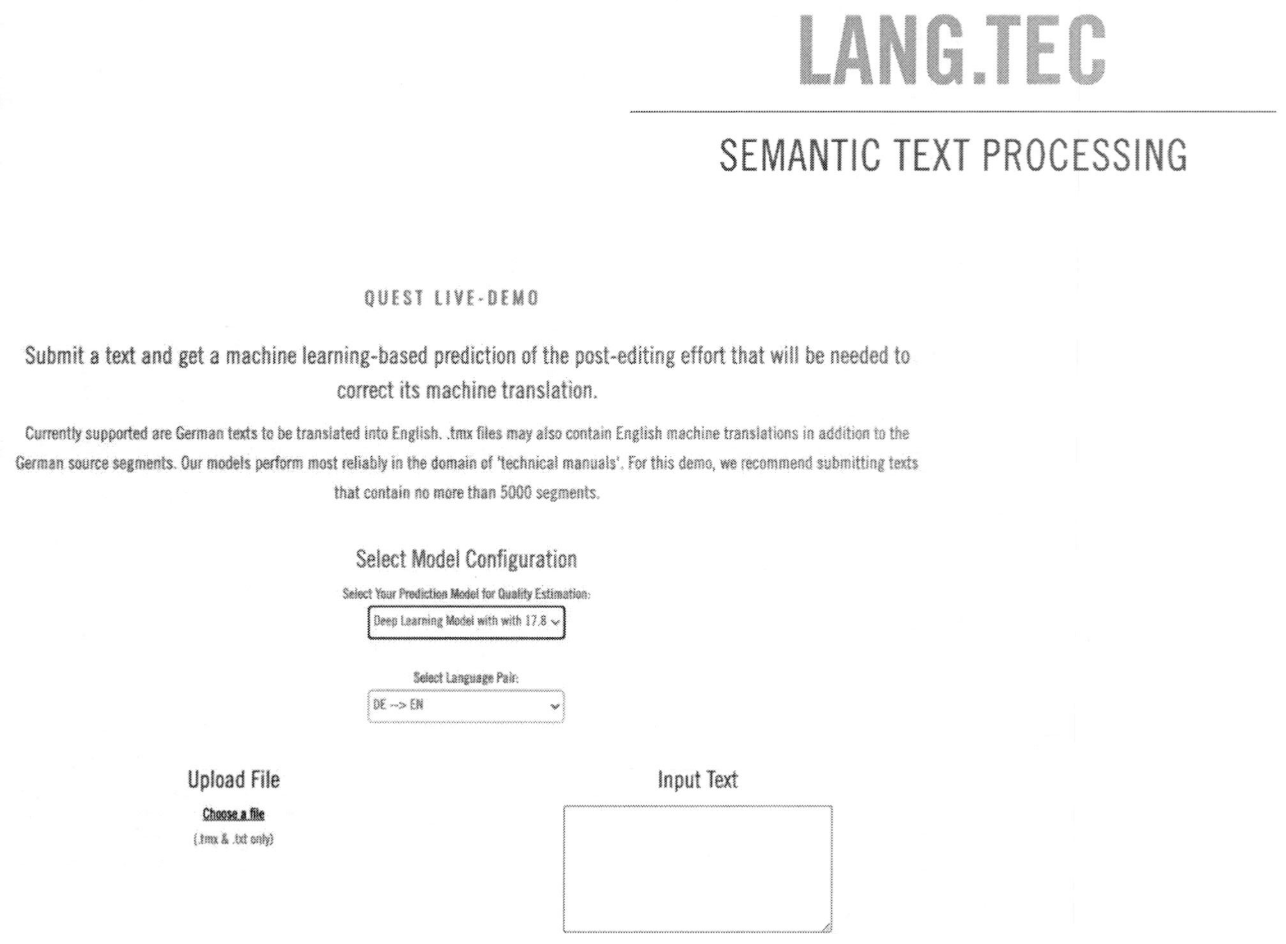

QUEST LIVE-DEMO

Submit a text and get a machine learning-based prediction of the post-editing effort that will be needed to correct its machine translation.

Currently supported are German texts to be translated into English. .tmx files may also contain English machine translations in addition to the German source segments. Our models perform most reliably in the domain of 'technical manuals'. For this demo, we recommend submitting texts that contain no more than 5000 segments.

Select Model Configuration

Select Your Prediction Model for Quality Estimation:

Deep Learning Model with with 17.8 ⌄

Select Language Pair:

DE --> EN

Upload File

Choose a file

(.tmx & .txt only)

Input Text

Different PE effort estimations

Proceedings of the 14th Conference of the Association for Machine Translation in the Americas
October 6 - 9, 20.   rkshop on Post-Editing in Modern-Day Translation

Model architecture

LANG.TEC

SEMANTIC TEXT PROCESSING

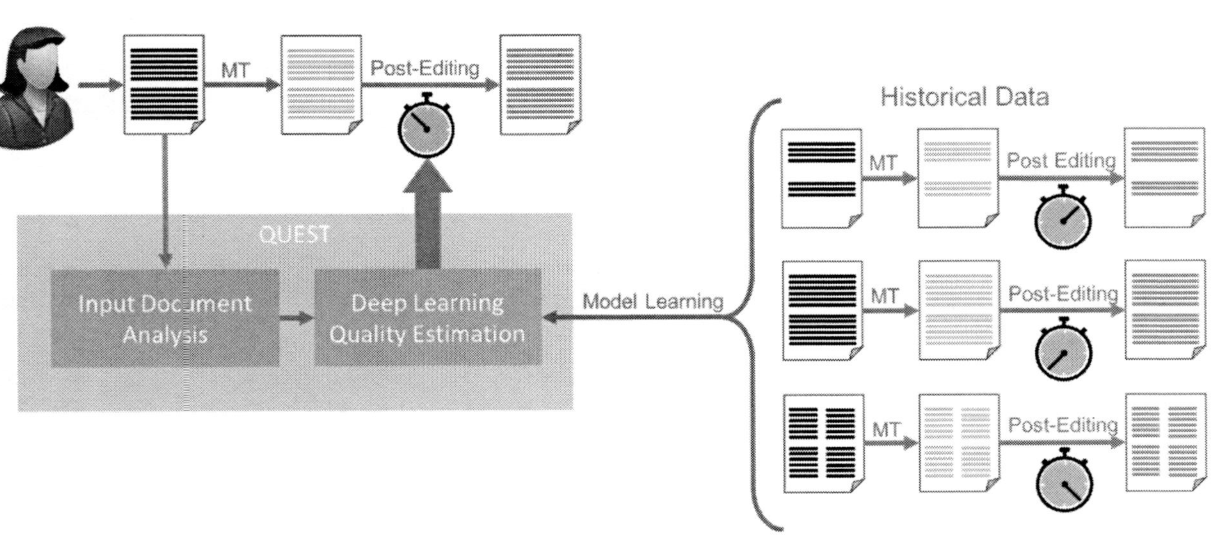

Proceedings of the 14th Conference of the Association for Machine Translation in the Americas
October 6 – 9, 20:   rkshop on Post–Editing in Modern–Day Translation

QUEST's usage contexts

1. Post-Edit Effort Prediction

2. MT-Recommendation Tool

3. MT-Profiling Tool

4. MT Quality Document Sorting

5. MT Quality Threshold Plug-In

Proceedings of the 14th Conference of the Association for Machine Translation in the Americas
October 6 – 9, 20:   rkshop on Post-Editing in Modern-Day Translation

Parting words

LANG.TEC

SEMANTIC TEXT PROCESSING

- QUEST can be used on-premise or in the cloud and custom models can be built within hours.

- Our machine learning model also scales to any language pair

- QUEST works as solution for leveraging MT for lesser-resourced languages

- LangTec can provide a free customized trial QUEST model for interested parties

Proceedings of the 14th Conference of the Association for Machine Translation in the Americas
October 6 – 9, 20:   rkshop on Post-Editing in Modern-Day Translation

Thank you!

LangTec

Dr. Christopher Reid
Associate Product Owner QUEST

Bundesstraße 28 a
20146 Hamburg
Germany

Phone: +49 . 40 . 180 610 98
E-mail: *christopher.reid@langtec.de*
Web: www.langtec.de

*Proceedings of the 14th Conference of the Association for Machine Translation in the Americas
October 6 – 9, 20:   rkshop on Post-Editing in Modern-Day Translation*

LANG.TEC

SEMANTIC TEXT PROCESSING

Proceedings of the 14th Conference of the Association for Machine Translation in the Americas
October 6 - 9, 20.   rkshop on Post-Editing in Modern-Day Translation

MT Post Editing challenges: Training happy and successful posteditors.

Abstract

Today, we can state that machine translation post-editing has replaced traditional human translation assignments for many linguists, and great deals of translators are actually working, successfully or not, as posteditors. No doubt, this trend has been constantly increasing and it will continue doing so exponentially. If we focus on the posteditor's environment, even those who are successful and proficient posteditors have not received formal training on MTPE as part as their academic background. Sound and organized training on postediting and guided practice based on production goals and results are key components of the translator's toolkit to attain quality and quantity expectations, and also happiness while doing their work. This training should mingle diverse skills, such as learning about technologies for MT deployment and linguistic resources for MT engine training, tools and guidelines for estimating quality and attainable outputs, industry standards for MT, such as ISO, and structured feedback to increase productivity and improve MT raw output.

In this presentation, I will focus on the relevant skills and tools that linguist/translators need to become productive posteditors and reliable auditors for MT raw output and content suitability, based on its domains and linguistic characteristics. This learning environment should set clear goals and steps from the technical, linguistic and strategy perspectives, as well as raise broader awareness of automatic evaluation and quality estimation, corpus management and engine training. Posteditors should be trained so as to support all the players in the MTPE service chain, from content creators, translation salesforce, project managers and actual posteditors and reviewers of MT postedited content.

This presentation aims at setting the basis for formal academic training at translation colleges and certification institutions.

MT Post Editing challenges: Training happy and successful posteditors.

Postediting demands

Postediting requests have exponentially increased in the recent years, and most large language companies have massively changed their assignments from translation into postediting, as end clients and developers have learned about the advantages that Artificial Intelligence has brought to them in terms of time to foreign markets and translated content versus zero translation.

Empowerment and knowledge

Knowledge is power… Feeling comfortable with the task, understanding the underlying technology and making posteditors (PE) aware of the authority they have on certain areas or links of the production chain make them more involved and willing to work harder and in a more effective way when needed to attain an optimal output. Even though not all postediting tasks are performed by professional translators, translation courses should include this subject as part of their curriculum or at least as an extension course or postgraduate seminar.

Main aspects to be taken into account include the following:

Posteditor's profile

Translation background - Is a translation degree required?

Experience as a proofer / translator: The fact that many translators only accept translation as their working assignments should be taken into account, as proofing experience and skills may be relevant for optimal performance.

Technical background – Do posteditors have a good command of the different tools and mechanical processes that are involved in the postediting assignment? (Namely, terminology management, TM integration, basic programming skills, for macros, regular expressions, etc.). Are they familiar with chatbots and Artificial intelligence (AI)?

Basic Project Managenent – Can posteditors create and manage their own projects, with all the components needed to automatize terminology, checks, updates, unique segments, splitting or slicing projects taking internal repetitions/matches into account, etc.?

Subject r   :er specialization – Equally relevant as for Human Translation (HT)

Training posteditors has become a challenge for institutions which in most part of the world have only recently started covering CAT tools. Well-organized curricula should include

Companies salesforces and Project managers unaware of the posteditor skills or unable to empower posteditors: frustration

Introduction to Machine Translation (MT) and postediting

MT-related terms and definitions

MT history (main hallmarks regarding MT types): from statistic-based to neural and adaptive

Analysis of several types of engines – how they are trained, fed, and how raw output is assessed

Output error identification – Clear taxonomy of the types of expected errors, including linguistic, formatting and technical potential issues, and their proposed fixing strategies. Text linguistics

Content type analysis: MT raw output varies by content and text genre

ISO as a framework or TAUS guidelines as a roadmap – Standards and industry-based procedures and recommendations as a scaffold for PE training

MT technologies and related tool

Pre-PE and Post-PE steps - Controlled language and authoring, monolingual proofreading, cultural validation, formatting

Sampling guidelines for MT raw output and strategic decision – What is going to be light-postedited; what is going to be full-postedited and what is going to be outsourced based on the traditional human translation/editing /proofing (TEP) model

Actual postediting

Job requirements for the assignment should be clearly described and outcome expectations should be thoroughly set forth in advance, including the steps and strategies that correlate with them. Mostly, the following should be covered:

Level of postediting: light vs. full; user requirements, PE buyer's information, purpose and nature of the product/content object of the language transfer, and any other assignment-related particulars

Terminology management

Concepts of over-edits/under-edits – If the PE is used to self-edit his/her work as a translator (HT) or proofing, a clear limit to where edits should end should be clearly defined

MT workflow, including structured feedback

Expected quality – Industry-based, client-based, product type-based, and quality assessment of raw output

Checklists – To reinforce Quality metrics

Self-productivity assessment: time an quality metrics; mental concentration.

Delta comparisons: PE should occasionally assess their performance comparing again their own HT productivity, when applicable.

Procedui   and practice

The actual steps to be taken for the postediting assignment should be depicted, with a detailed description of the procedures and tools involves, as well as the "on-focus" skills for carrying out each of them.

2-Layer postediting (Bilingual postediting focused on accuracy + target only, focused on fluency and language (grammar/syntax, punctuation, spelling, etc.)

OR,

Full bilingual postediting, with or without a separate proofing step (like in HT, performed by another linguist)

Mechanical checks: black lists, advanced terminology management, regex, macros, consistency checks, etc.

Bilingual / Target only checks and fixing strategies

Hands-on Practice: from modular practical training (meaning, stepwise separation of tasks: raw output assessment, error taxonomy, text linguistics, etc.) to comprehensive postediting, covering the different content types, communicative purposes, participants and situations

Improve productivity – Is a better productivity attained in terms of speed, hourly rates, quality at large?

Conclusion

For optimal results, these curricula or programs should be designed as a multidisciplinary effort including linguists/language experts, subject matter experts (SME), MT trainers/developers, and terminologists. Training should be mostly practical, based on examples and the level of complexity of the content as well as the degree of requirements should be gradually increased, as for any other training environment. Academia and industry players should work together to set their goals, needs and expectations in order to reproduce a real-world scenario in the training workflow.

References

ISO 18587 Translation services — Post-editing of machine translation output — Requirements. First edition

2017-04

Guerberof Arenas, A, Moorkens, Joss. Machine translation and post-editing training as part of a master's programme. The Journal of Specialised Translation, Issue 31 – January 2019. Available at: https://www.jostrans.org/issue31/art_guerberof.pdf
TAUS (Translation Automation User Society). Evaluating Post-Editor Performance Guidelines. First published, February 2014. Available at: https://www.taus.net/academy/best-practices/postedit-best-practices/evaluating-post-editor-performance-guidelines

TAUS (Translation Automation User Society). MT Post-Editing Guidelines. First published, November 2010. Available at: https://www.taus.net/academy/best-practices/postedit-best-practices/machine-translation-post-editing-guidelines

TAUS (Translation Automation User Society). Post-Editing Productivity Guidelines. First published, Decembe)12. Available at: https://www.taus.net/academy/best-practices/postedit-best-practices   st-editing-productivity

Luciana Ramos's abridged bio

Luciana Ramos is a professional translator and interpreter with a long-standing presence in the Language and Technology industry, which, based on her sound linguistic background, broad experience in every link of the translation and localization supply chain (both as a linguist and a businesswoman), her specialist knowledge on language technologies and her research capabilities, offers a comprehensive array of professional services: scientific translation, software localization, telephone/on-site interpreting, professional training and coaching (for translators, vendor managers and project managers), as well as consulting on business organization and processes, Quality Assurance, and investments on technology.

Luciana Ramos holds a Master Degree on Biomedical Translation from the Universitat Jaume I, Castellon, Spain, and a Technical-scientific and Literary Translator Degree for English into Spanish, and Consecutive and Simultaneous Interpreter Degree, both issued by Instituto de Enseñanza Superior "Olga Cossettini" Rosario, Argentina; 1992-1996. She has also been certified by the American Translators Association for English into Spanish Translations. As a member of Colegio de Traductores de la Pcia. de Santa Fe (2.º circunscrip.), Luciana Ramos does business under Professional License # 218/02. As a source of continuing education, market trends and business developments, Luciana is a proud member of Tremédica, GALA and ATA. Luciana has delivered, for international audiences, webinars, in-person workshops and courses, and conference presentations on several fields related to translation specialization and technology, with an important focus on Machine translation.

Proceedings of the 14th Conference of the Association for Machine Translation in the Americas
October 6 – 9, 2020, 1st Workshop on Post-Editing in Modern-Day Translation

COPECO

We present a platform with three main objectives:

- Collecting post-edits produced by students and teacher corrections

- Building an open-source student post-editing corpus

- Make more systematic the task of translation error annotation

COPECO

Proceedings of the 14th Conference of the Association for Machine Translation in the Americas
October 6 - 9, 2020, 1st Workshop on Post-Editing in Modern-Day Translation

- Correcting could be tedious

- Sharing annotation schemes

- Recycling texts and references

- Illustrating different post-editing processes (monolingual, bilingual, source first, machine translation first, segment by segments)

- Have an online pedagogical tool to correct post-edits

UNIVERSITÉ DE GENÈVE
FACULTÉ DE TRADUCTION ET D'INTERPRÉTATION

LIÈGE université

COPECO

Proceedings of the 14th Conference of the Association for Machine Translation in the Americas
October 6 – 9, 2020, 1st Workshop on Post-Editing in Modern-Day Translation

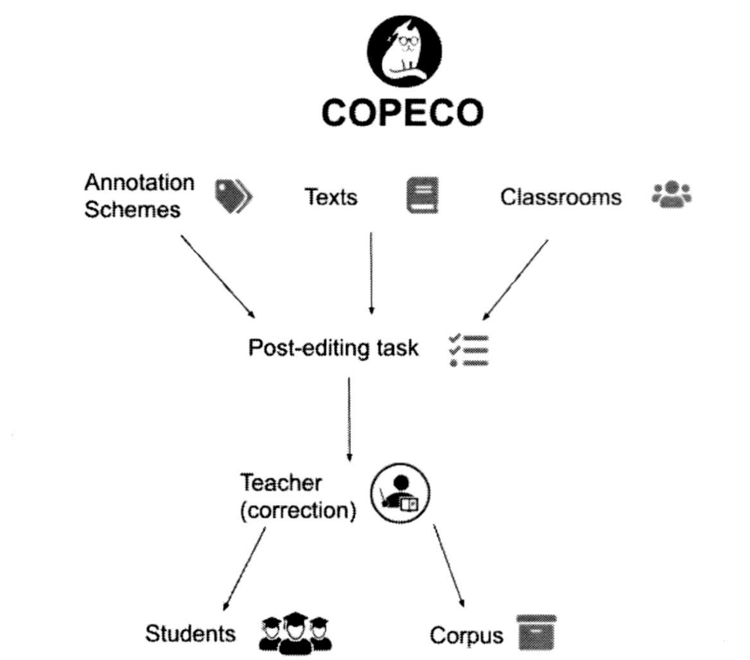

How?
UNIVERSITÉ DE GENÈVE
FACULTÉ DE TRADUCTION ET D'INTERPRÉTATION
LIÈGE université

COPECO
Annotation Schemes
Texts
Classrooms
Post-editing task
Teacher (correction)
Students
Corpus
COPECO
https://copeco.unige.ch/

COPECO

A Collaborative Post-Editing Corpus in Pedagogical Context

OBJECTIVES

Proceedings of the 14th Conference of the Association for Machine Translation in the Americas
October 6 – 9, 2020, 1st Workshop on Post-Editing in Modern-Day Translation

Annotation Schemes

List

Annotation Scheme Title	Description	Import
MQM →	Multidimensional Quality … (see more)	Imported
An extra Schema →	Bla bla … (see more)	Imported
General Schema to personalize	Import this schema if you … (see more)	Import
Mathilde Fontanet ↓	Grille FTI … (see more)	Imported
Traduction_Contresens (CS)	Choix d'un mot ou d'une e … (see more)	
Traduction_Fauxsens (FS)	Choix d'un mot ou d'une e … (see more)	
Traduction_Glissementdesens (GL)	Altération mineure du sen … (see more)	
Traduction_Omissions (OM)	Omission correspondant à … (see more)	
Traduction_Ambiguïté (AM)	Phrase ambiguë. … (see more)	
Traduction_AjoutInjustifié (AJ)	Ajout injustifié. … (see more)	
Langue_Grammaire_syntaxeFautive (SYN)	Syntaxe Fautive … (see more)	
Langue_Grammaire_TempsVerbal (TPS)	Temps verbal ou mode inad … (see more)	
Langue_Grammaire_Accord (ACC)	Accord fautif … (see more)	

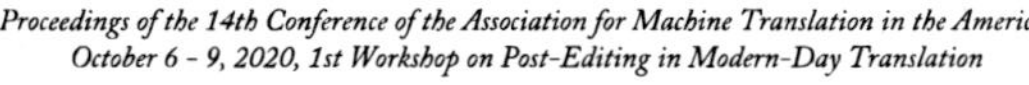

Annotation Schemes

Proceedings of the 14th Conference of the Association for Machine Translation in the Americas
October 6 - 9, 2020, 1st Workshop on Post-Editing in Modern-Day Translation

UNIVERSITÉ DE GENÈVE
FACULTÉ DE TRADUCTION ET D'INTERPRÉTATION

LIÈGE université

Tags for correction

List

Correction Scheme	Description		
An extra Schema →	Bla bla more...	Add New Tag ⊕	🗑
MQM ⬇	Multidimensional Quality more...	Add New Tag ⊕	🗑
accuracy	The target text does not accurately reflect the source text, allowing for any differences authorized by specifications.	▨	✎ ǀ 🗑
verity.completeness	The text is incomplete	▨	✎ ǀ 🗑
verity	The text makes statements that contradict the world of the text	▨	✎ ǀ 🗑
terminology	A term (domain-specific word) is translated with a term other than the one expected for the domain or otherwise specified.	▨	✎ ǀ 🗑
style	The text has stylistic problems.	▨	✎ ǀ 🗑
locale-convention	The text does not adhere to locale-specific mechanical conventions and violates requirements for the presentation of content in the target locale.	▨	✎ ǀ 🗑

Annotation Schemes

Proceedings of the 14th Conference of the Association for Machine Translation in the Americas
October 6 – 9, 2020, 1st Workshop on Post-Editing in Modern-Day Translation

The Collaborative Economy Disrupts Existing Institutions

Align text

Name	Domain	MTSystem	MTSystemDate	OriginReference	Reference?	Is Aligned?
The Collaborative Economy Disrupts Existing Institutions	Economy	DeepL	29.09.2020 00:00:00	Wikipedia	✕	✓

Source

The Collaborative Economy Disrupts Existing Institutions

The Collaborative Economy is disruptive to existing institutions as businesses become disintermediated by customers who are empowered to transact directly with each other. These examples illustrate disruptions that are already taking place

Transportation

Buy one car, share many times. Commuters have long relied on "casual carpool" for informal, ad-hoc carpooling. This model has birthed a new crop of car-sharing businesses, from Lyft (peer to peer "taxis"), RelayRide (peer-to-peer car rental), and Carpooling.com (rideshare). A University of California study found that every car-sharing vehicle replaces 9-13 vehicles,10 reducing the number of hours a car sits idle in a garage or parking lot and car ownership overall.

Products & Apparel

Product rentals and exchanges over purchases. Today, Chegg and Bookcrossing allow students to exchange or rent books with each other. Fashionistas can wear the latest trends by renting clothing and accessories through sites like Bag, Borrow or Steal, and Rent the Runway — or

Machine Translation

L'économie collaborative perturbe les institutions existantes

L'économie collaborative perturbe les institutions existantes car les entreprises sont désintermédiées par les clients qui sont habilités à effectuer des transactions directement entre eux. Ces exemples illustrent les perturbations qui se produisent déjà

Transport

Achetez une voiture, partagez plusieurs fois. Les navetteurs ont longtemps compté sur le "covoiturage occasionnel" pour le covoiturage informel et ponctuel. Ce modèle a donné naissance à une nouvelle génération d'entreprises de covoiturage, de Lyft (taxis "peer to peer"), RelayRide (location de voitures peer-to-peer) et Carpooling.com (covoiturage). Une étude de l'Université de Californie a révélé que chaque véhicule partagé remplace 9 à 13 véhicules10, ce qui réduit le nombre d'heures d'immobilisation d'une voiture dans un garage ou un parking et le nombre de propriétaires de voitures en général.

Produits et vêtements

Location et échange de produits sur achats. Aujourd'hui, Chegg et Bookcrossing permettent aux étudiants d'échanger ou de louer des livres

Text

Proceedings of the 14th Conference of the Association for Machine Translation in the Americas
October 6 - 9, 2020, 1st Workshop on Post-Editing in Modern-Day Translation

Classroom

Create

Classroom name

Select file to include emails from students:

Browse... No file selected.

If you don't have any file, please create the classroom and then you can manually add the students.

Create   Download example file

Back to List

Proceedings of the 14th Conference of the Association for Machine Translation in the Americas
October 6 - 9, 2020, 1st Workshop on Post-Editing in Modern-Day Translation

Post-editing Task

Create

Task Name

The Collaborative Economy Task

Task Type

Show source and target (Bilingual post-editing)

Select classroom ✛

CL

Tags for correction

MQM

Texts ✛

The Collaborative Economy Disrupts Existing Institutions

Split the text into segments? ☑

❗The text will not be split into segments if you haven't manually done the aligment.

Create New Task

back to list

UNIVERSITÉ DE GENÈVE
FACULTÉ DE TRADUCTION ET D'INTERPRÉTATION

LIÈGE université

Post-Editing tasks: Create

Proceedings of the 14th Conference of the Association for Machine Translation in the Americas
October 6 - 9, 2020, 1st Workshop on Post-Editing in Modern-Day Translation

My post-editing Tasks

Name	Teacher Email	Created	Status	Task Type	Ready?
The Collaborative Economy Task - All Text	manager@gmail.com	06.10.2020	Post-edit	showAll	Submit
The Collaborative Economy Task	manager@gmail.com	06.10.2020	Post-edit	hideSource	Submit
Name 1	manager@gmail.com	28.09.2020	Corrections	showAll	Submitted
QES texte 2	schumacher.perrine@gmail.com	28.09.2020	Post-edit	hideTarget	Submit

Post-Editing tasks: Post-edit

UNIVERSITÉ DE GENÈVE
FACULTÉ DE TRADUCTION ET D'INTERPRÉTATION

LIÈGE université

The Collaborative Economy Task - All Text

Return to the task list

The Collaborative Economy Disrupts Existing Institutions	L'économie collaborative perturbe les institutions existantes
The Collaborative Economy is disruptive to existing institutions as businesses become disintermediated by customers who are empowered to transact directly with each other. These examples illustrate disruptions that are already taking place	L'économie collaborative perturbe les institutions existantes car les entreprises sont désintermédiées par les clients qui sont habilités à effectuer des transactions directement entre eux. Ces exemples illustrent les perturbations qui se produisent déjà
Transportation	Transport
Buy one car, share many times. Commuters have long relied on "casual carpool" for informal, ad-hoc carpooling. This model has birthed a new crop of car-sharing businesses, from Lyft (peer to peer "taxis"), RelayRide (peer-to-peer car rental), and Carpooling.com (rideshare). A University of California study found that every car-sharing vehicle replaces 9-13 vehicles,10 reducing the number of hours a car sits idle in a garage or parking lot and car ownership overall	Achetez une voiture, partagez plusieurs fois. Les navetteurs ont longtemps compté sur le "covoiturage occasionnel" pour le covoiturage informel et ponctuel. Ce modèle a donné naissance à une nouvelle génération d'entreprises de covoiturage, de Lyft (taxis "peer to peer"), RelayRide (location de voitures peer-to-peer) et Carpooling.com (covoiturage). Une étude de l'Université de Californie a révélé que chaque véhicule partagé remplace 9 à 13 véhicules10, ce qui réduit le nombre d'heures d'immobilisation d'une voiture dans un garage ou un parking et le nombre de propriétaires de voitures en général.
Products & Apparel	Produits et vêtements
Product rentals and exchanges over purchases. Today, Chegg and Bookcrossing allow students to exchange or rent books with each other. Fashionistas can wear the latest trends by renting clothing and accessories through sites like Bag, Borrow or Steal, and Rent the Runway — or swapping clothes on 99dresses for an "infinite closet of free fashion." From consumer electronics on UseSold.com to children's toys on Toyswap, consumers can now rent or exchange any number of physical goods instead of buying them from traditional retailers.	Location et échange de produits sur achats. Aujourd'hui, Chegg et Bookcrossing permettent aux étudiants d'échanger ou de louer des livres entre eux. Les fashionistas peuvent porter les dernières tendances en louant des vêtements et des accessoires sur des sites comme Bag, Borrow or Steal, et Rent the Runway - ou en échangeant des vêtements sur 99dresses contre un "placard infini de mode gratuite". De l'électronique grand public sur UseSold.com aux jouets pour enfants sur Toyswap, les consommateurs peuvent désormais louer ou échanger un nombre illimité de biens physiques au lieu de les acheter chez les détaillants traditionnels.
Hospitality	Hospitalité
Homeowners displace hotels. The oldest known hotel in Japan, the Nisiyama Onsen Keiunkan, which opened in 707 A.D. has been operated by the same family for 46 generations. Now, Airbnb users can "monetize their extra space" by renting out rooms or homes to travelers from around the world. For the luxury-inclined, onefinestay connects renters with owners of upscale homes in London. And members of HomeExchange swap their homes for a nominal fee. Travelers can now bypass hotels for more unique, affordable, or even convenient travel experiences.	Les propriétaires déplacent les hôtels. Le plus ancien hôtel connu au Japon, le Nisiyama Onsen Keiunkan, qui a ouvert ses portes en 707 après J.-C., est exploité par la même famille depuis 46 générations. Aujourd'hui, les utilisateurs d'Airbnb peuvent "monétiser leur espace supplémentaire" en louant des chambres ou des maisons à des voyageurs du monde
Office Rental	

Task with full text

The Collaborative Economy Task

Return to the task list

Show Source	
Show Source	
Show Source	
Buy one car, share many times. Commuters have long relied on "casual carpool" for informal, ad-hoc carpooling. This model has birthed a new crop of car-sharing businesses, from Lyft (peer to peer "taxis"), RelayRide (peer-to-peer car rental), and Carpooling.com (rideshare). A University of California study found that every car-sharing vehicle replaces 9-13 vehicles,10 reducing the number of hours a car sits idle in a garage or parking lot and car ownership overall.	Achetez une voiture, partagez plusieurs fois. Les navetteurs ont longtemps compté sur le "covoiturage occasionnel" pour le covoiturage informel et ponctuel. Ce modèle a donné naissance à une nouvelle génération d'entreprises de covoiturage, de Lyft (taxis "peer to peer"), RelayRide (location de voitures peer-to-peer) et Carpooling.com (covoiturage). Une étude de l'Université de Californie a révélé que chaque véhicule partagé remplace 9 à 13 véhicules10, ce qui réduit le nombre d'heures d'immobilisation d'une voiture dans un garage ou un parking et le nombre de propriétaires de voitures en général.

Task segment by segment

Post-Editing tasks: Post-edit

Segments to correct

Return to pending corrections

Information

Task Type hideSource

Student Email student@gmail.com

Tags for Correction

Show Tags

Segment 510

Words	Avg Secs per Word	Total time to edit	Number of key strokes
32	0,57s	18,44s	10

Source	The Collaborative Economy is disruptive to existing institutions as businesses become disintermediated by customers who are empowered to transact directly with each other. These examples illustrate disruptions that are already taking place
Machine Translation	L'économie collaborative perturbe les institutions existantes ca[...]s par les clients qui sont habilités à effectuer des transactions directement entre eux. Ces exemples illustrent les perturbations qui se produisent déjà
Target	L'économie collaborative bouleverse les modèles existants ; les [...]diaire aux clients, car ces derniers sont en mesure de négocier directement les uns avec les autres. Ces exemples illustrent les transformations déjà observables :
Correction	L'économie collaborative bouleverse les modèles existants ; les entreprises ne servent plus d'intermédiaire aux clients, car ces derniers sont en mesure de négocier directement les uns avec les autres. Ces exemples illustrent les transformations déjà observables :

Comments...

Add tags.

Type in a search term

Cancel   Save

Previous   Next

UNIVERSITÉ DE GENÈVE
FACULTÉ DE TRADUCTION ET D'INTERPRÉTATION

LIÈGE université

Post-Editing tasks Correction

Proceedings of the 14th Conference of the Association for Machine Translation in the Americas
October 6 - 9, 2020, 1st Workshop on Post-Editing in Modern-Day Translation

Segments

Source	The Collaborative Economy Disrupts Existing Institutions
Machine Translation	L'économie collaborative perturbe les institutions existantes
Correction	L'économie axée sur la collaboration perturbe les institutions existantes

Source	The Collaborative Economy is disruptive to existing institutions as businesses become disintermediated by customers who are empowered to transact directly with each other. These examples illustrate disruptions that are already taking place
Machine Translation	L'économie collaborative perturbe les institutions existantes car les entreprises sont désintermédiées par les clients qui sont habilités à effectuer des transactions directement entre eux. Ces exemples illustrent les perturbations qui se produisent déjà
Correction	L'économie collaborative perturbe les institutions existantes car les entreprises sont désintermédiées par des clients qui sont habilités à transiger directement les uns avec les autres. Ces exemples illustrent les perturbations qui se produisent déjà

Source	Products & Apparel
Machine Translation	Produits et vêtements
Correction	Produits et vêtements

Source	Product rentals and exchanges over purchases. Today, Chegg and Bookcrossing allow students to exchange or rent books with each other. Fashionistas can wear the latest trends by renting clothing and accessories through sites like Bag, Borrow or Steal, and Rent the Runway — or swapping clothes on 99dresses for an "infinite closet of free fashion." From consumer electronics on UseSold.com to children's toys on Toyswap, consumers can now rent or exchange any number of physical goods instead of buying them from traditional retailers.
Machine Translation	Location et échange de produits sur achats. Aujourd'hui, Chegg et Bookcrossing permettent aux étudiants d'échanger ou de louer des livres entre eux. Les fashionistas peuvent porter les dernières tendances en louant des vêtements et des accessoires sur des sites comme Bag, Borrow or Steal. et Rent the Runway - ou échangeant des vêtements sur 99dresses contre un "placard infini de mode gratuite". De l'électronique grand public sur UseSold.com aux jouets pour enfants sur Toyswap, les consommateurs peuvent désormais louer ou échanger un nombre illimité de biens physiques au lieu de les acheter chez les détaillants traditionnels.
Correction	La location et l'échange de produits sur les achats. Aujourd'hui,Chegg et Bookcrossing permettent aux étudiants d'échanger ou de louer des livres entre eux. Les fashionistas peuvent porter les dernières tendances en louant des vêtements et des accessoires sur des sites comme Borrow or Steal, et Rent the Runway - ou en échangeant des vêtements sur 99 adresses contre un "placard infini de mode libre". De l'électronique grand public sur UseSold.com aux jouets pour enfants sur Toyswap, les consommateurs peuvent désormais louer ou échanger n'importe quel nombre de biens physiques au lieu de les acheter chez les détaillants traditionnels.

Post-Editing Tasks Corrections

Post-editing Tasks ➕

List

Name	Creation Date	Schema tags for correction	Task Type	
The Collaborative Economy Task - All Text »	06.10.2020 05:04:39	MQM	showAll	🗑
The Collaborative Economy Task »	06.10.2020 05:04:00	Mathilde Fontanet	hideSource	🗑
Name 1 »	28.09.2020 15:10:05	Mathilde Fontanet	showAll	🗑
Task name 1 »	24.09.2020 09:44:43	MQM	showAll	🗑

← Post-editing Tasks

List

Post-Editing Name	Student Email	Share ⓘ	Status	
The Collaborative Economy Task	jonathan_mutal@hotmail.com	⤴	Waiting for student	🗑
The Collaborative Economy Task	student@gmail.com	⤴	To Correct	🗑

Back to all post-editing task

Corpus: Sharing

Proceedings of the 14th Conference of the Association for Machine Translation in the Americas
October 6 – 9, 2020, 1st Workshop on Post-Editing in Modern-Day Translation

Available Corpora

Name	Task Type	Creation Date	Student-id	Teacher-id	Is corrected?	
The Collaborative Economy Task	hideSource	06.10.2020 05:04:00	32ec	0718	✗	Details
Name 1	showAll	28.09.2020 15:10:05	32ec	0718	✔	Details
PE1	showAll	26.08.2020 10:11:42	32ec	a08d	✔	Details
PE1	showAll	26.08.2020 10:11:42	4db3	a08d	✗	Details
PE1	showAll	26.08.2020 10:11:42	ef65	a08d	✗	Details

Corpus

Proceedings of the 14th Conference of the Association for Machine Translation in the Americas
October 6 - 9, 2020, 1st Workshop on Post-Editing in Modern-Day Translation

Errors

Hide Tags

Name	Color	Description	#Error
Fluidité (calque, idiomaticité, registre, répétition)		- Calque lexical ou calque syntaxique - Idiomaticité : Construction grammaticalement correcte mais il y a un problème d'idiomaticité : Mauvaise cooccurrence, tournure non idiomatique, collocation malheureuse, lourdeur, déformation de proverbes... - Répétition : Un même mot/expression ou un mot/expression similaire est employé(e) trop souvent ou est trop proche de l'occurrence précédente de ce mot/expression. - Registre : Registre jugé trop formel/informel pour le contexte - Longueur de phrase: Phrase trop longue ou trop courte - Etc.	8
Ponctuation		Faute de ponctuation, signe manquant ou superflu.	2
Vocabulaire		- Inadéquation Terme inadéquat - Barbarisme et impropriété Barbarisme : Forme d'un mot qui n'existe pas en français ; déformation d'un mot, faute de conjugaison. Ex. : « abrévier » pour « abréger » ; « il envoira » pour « il enverra » Impropriété : Utilisation d'un mot existant mais selon une acception qu'il n'a pas. Ex. : « recouvrir la vue » plutôt que « recouvrer la vue » -Régionalisme Belgicisme, québécisme, etc. jugé fautif ou inapproprié dans ce contexte.	2
Non-sens		« Faute de traduction qui consiste à attribuer à un segment du texte de départ un sens erroné qui a pour effet d'introduire dans le texte d'arrivée une formulation absurde » (Delisle 2013 : 672)	4
Typographie/Coquille		Faute typographique (omission, inversion, substitution de lettres, etc.)	3
Omission		"Faute de traduction qui consiste à ne pas rendre dans le texte d'arrivée un élément de sens du texte de départ sans raison valable." (Delisle 2013 : 673)	1

Hide chart

Corpus: Corrections

Proceedings of the 14th Conference of the Association for Machine Translation in the Americas
October 6 - 9, 2020, 1st Workshop on Post-Editing in Modern-Day Translation

Q&A/Suggestions

Proceedings of the 14th Conference of the Association for Machine Translation in the Americas
October 6 – 9, 2020, 1st Workshop on Post-Editing in Modern-Day Translation

MT for Subtitling: Investigating professional translators' user experience and feedback

Maarit Koponen   maarit.koponen@helsinki.fi
Department of Digital Humanities, HELDIG, University of Helsinki, Helsinki, Finland

Umut Sulubacak   umut.sulubacak@helsinki.fi
Department of Digital Humanities, HELDIG, University of Helsinki, Helsinki, Finland

Kaisa Vitikainen   kaisa.vitikainen@yle.fi
Yleisradio Oy, Helsinki, Finland

Jörg Tiedemann   jorg.tiedemann@helsinki.fi
Department of Digital Humanities, HELDIG, University of Helsinki, Helsinki, Finland

Abstract

This paper presents a study of machine translation and post-editing in the field of audiovisual translation. We analyse user experience data collected from post-editing tasks completed by twelve translators in four language pairs. We also present feedback provided by the translators in semi-structured interviews. The results of the user experience survey and thematic analysis of interviews shows that the translators' impression of post-editing subtitles was on average neutral to somewhat negative, with segmentation and timing of subtitles identified as a key factor. Finally, we discuss the implications of the issues arising from the user experience survey and interviews for the future development of automatic subtitle translation.

1   Introduction

Developments in translation technology and machine translation (MT), particularly the quality improvements achieved by neural machine translation (NMT) in recent years, have led to MT increasingly becoming part of the modern-day translators' toolkit. Although post-editing (PE), where MT is used to produce a raw translation output which is then checked and corrected by a translator, has increased in many areas of translation, its use remains uncommon in audiovisual translation (AVT). AVT approaches include dubbing, voice-overs and subtitling for the purpose of making AV content accessible to audiences with no or limited understanding of the language of the original content. Different approaches are used to varying degrees depending on the type of content (e.g. voice-overs are common for documentaries) and region (e.g. subtitling is the predominant practice in Northern European countries).

As studies and practical experience have shown potential for PE in increasing productivity in other forms of translation, interest in implementing MT tools and PE workflows has also grown in the AV field. Studies have explored the use of MTPE subtitle translation with some promising although mixed results regarding effect on productivity (e.g. Bywood et al., 2017). When exploring the usability of such tools, however, productivity measurement is only one aspect. As Etchegoyhen et al. (2014) argue, subjective feedback from translators is equally important, as it provides insight into the actual user experience and necessary improvements.

This paper presents a pilot study investigating the usability of MT and PE in the subtitling workflow from the perspective of the prospective users. Twelve professional subtitle translators working in four language pairs (Finnish↔Swedish and Finnish↔English) subtitled short video clips by post-editing MT output. We analyse feedback collected with a user experience questionnaire and semi-structured interviews for positive and negative evaluations of the PE experience and improvement suggestions. We start with an overview of related work on MT and PE in the subtitling context and work on user feedback (Section 2). After describing our approach to automatic subtitle translation (Section 3), and the subtitle PE experiment (Section 4), we present the questionnaire and interview analyses (Section 5), followed by discussion of the observations and our ongoing work based on these analyses.

2 Related work

2.1 Subtitling, MT and PE

Subtitle translation differs from translating purely textual material in that the source text consists of the spoken audio, together with the visual mode, while the target text is a written representation of translated speech. Due to technical limitations like the number of characters within a subtitle frame and the time each subtitle remains visible, paraphrasing and condensation are typical features of subtitle translation (see e.g. Pedersen, 2017). The work of subtitle translators may involve "first translation", where they translate from the source audio and determine the segmentation and timing of the subtitle frames ("spotting"), or translation with subtitle templates, where the source text consists of pre-existing intralingual subtitles in the source language or sometimes interlingual subtitles in a pivot language (often English) with set subtitle segmentation and timing (Nikolić, 2015).

To date, the use of MT and PE for subtitling has been less common in AVT than other translation fields. Explanations for this may include the characteristics of subtitle translation, which pose challenges for MT, and also the difficulty of integrating current NMT systems to subtitle translation workflows (Matusov et al., 2019). MT for movie and TV subtitling has been tested in some language pairs since the early 2000s (Melero et al., 2006; Volk et al., 2010; de Sousa et al., 2011) with suggestions that PE may increase productivity also in this context.

A subtitle-oriented statistical MT system and PE platform was developed by the SUMAT project, and tested in a user evaluation involving several language pairs and 19 professional subtitle translators (Etchegoyhen et al., 2014; Bywood et al., 2017). In a study comparing task time for translation from scratch and MTPE, Bywood et al. (2017) report that MTPE increased the translators productivity; however, the results varied for different translators, language pairs and content types. More recently, Matusov et al. (2019) tested an NMT system customised for subtitles using parallel subtitle corpora from OpenSubtitles, GlobalVoices and TED talks and reported productivity increases for MTPE in a study involving two translators.

So far, work has focused on the use of intralingual subtitles as the source text for MT, but a recent paper by Karakanta et al. (2020a) explores an end-to-end spoken language translation system for subtitling. No user evaluation of the system is reported, although Karakanta et al. (2020a) note that based on automatic evaluation against "gold standard" human subtitles the MT quality appears satisfactory. Karakanta et al. (2020b) also investigate annotating subtitle corpora for segment breaks and propose an approach for segmenting sentences into subtitles conforming to length constraints.

2.2 Studies on user experience/feedback from translators

Subjective feedback is invaluable for providing insight into tools and workflows that affect the actual work of the prospective users, and revealing issues that would not be evident from the translations or process data (see Bundgaard, 2017). Various studies have investigated professional translators' experience with and perceptions of MT and PE with questionnaires and interviews. Analyses have reported mixed experiences: while translators sometimes find MT helpful, for example by providing useful terminology and making their work faster, other times PE may be even slower than translation from scratch. Whether working with technical or literary texts, translators often express concerns about MT affecting the final translation quality as well as their (cognitive) processes because the output can potentially mislead the translator or limit their creativity (e.g. Guerberof Arenas, 2013; Bundgaard, 2017; Moorkens et al., 2018).

Translator feedback on MT and PE in the context of AV translation was collected and analysed in the user evaluations of the SUMAT project (Etchegoyhen et al., 2014; Bywood et al., 2017). Etchegoyhen et al. (2014) describe a questionnaire used in the second evaluation round, where 19 translators carried out PE tasks in several language pairs and rated their impression of the PE process rather negatively overall (average 2.37 on a 5-point scale). Based on translator feedback, Etchegoyhen et al. (2014) identified improving MT quality to reduce cognitive load, improving quality estimation and filtering MT segments, and improving user interfaces for PE of MT subtitles as key issues for increasing usability.

Matusov et al. (2019) report a user experiment with two translators who both subtitled two programmes (a documentary and a sitcom) partly from scratch and partly with two different MT outputs. The translators rated their impression of the PE experience on average "fair" (3 on a 5-point scale) for the subtitle optimised system. The translator feedback noted useful terminology as one of the main reasons they would consider using MT in their work, but also expressed concerns about incorrect or unusual translations in the MT affecting the quality of the final translation (Matusov et al., 2019).

The study reported in this paper builds upon these analyses by collecting feedback on MT and PE for subtitling from professional subtitle translators. We aim to investigate the translators' impressions of PE more closely by introducing a more detailed user experience questionnaire where they rate different aspects of the process (see Section 4.3).

3 Automatic subtitle translation

Machine translation for subtitles requires some special treatment that we will discuss in this section. In particular, we consider models with extended context, which we will call *document-level translation models* and special tools that align translations with subtitle frames to be shown on screen. First, we briefly present the datasets and models before discussing frame alignment as a post-processing step.

3.1 Datasets and MT models

Our MT models are trained on a mix of diverse data sets[1] taken from OPUS.[2] Altogether, this includes over 30 million translation units for Finnish↔Swedish and about 44 million units for Finnish↔English. We follow the common practice in MT development to include as much data as possible even when coming from very different domains. However, the largest proportion of the training examples comes from a large collection of movie and TV show subtitles (the OpenSubtitles v2018 dataset) constituting almost half of the Finnish↔Swedish data and over 65% of the Finnish↔English data. This is certainly an advantage for our task and, hence, we expect a rather good domain-fit of our models.

We train both sentence-level and document-level models based on the Transformer architecture (Vaswani et al., 2017), the current state of the art in NMT. In particular, we apply the implementation from the MarianNMT toolkit (Junczys-Dowmunt et al., 2018), a production-ready software with fast training and decoding tools. The architecture refers to a 6-layered

---

[1]OPUS corpora used: bible-uedin, DGT, EMEA, EUbookshop, EUconst, Europarl, Finlex, fiskmo, GNOME, infopankki, JRC-Acquis, KDE4, MultiParaCrawl, OpenSubtitles, PHP, QED, Tatoeba, TildeMODEL, Ubuntu, wikimedia
[2]http://opus.nlpl.eu

network in both the encoder and decoder with 8 self-attention heads per layer. Recommended features like label smoothing and dropout are enabled and we use tied embeddings and a shared vocabulary. SentencePiece (Kudo and Richardson, 2018) is used for tokenisation and subword segmentation with models independently trained for source and target language. The shared vocabulary is set to a size of 65,000 with equal proportions in each language.

The document-level models refer to *concatenative models* proposed by Tiedemann and Scherrer (2017) and Junczys-Dowmunt (2019) using units of a maximum length of 100 tokens and special tokens for marking sentence boundaries. We observed that 100 tokens typically covers a substantial amount of contextual information in subtitles where sentences and sentence fragments are often very short. About 3.3 million pseudo-documents are created in a sequential way without overlaps for Finnish↔Swedish and 4.7 million pseudo-documents for Finnish↔English, corresponding to roughly 9 sentences per document on average.

The same kind of chunking needs to be done during test time. Sentence-level models are translated in the usual way. Note, however, that subtitles need to be pre-processed in a proper way in order to extract proper textual units that correspond to complete sentences to be translated. This involves merging fragments that run across subtitle frames and splitting frames in other cases.

We apply all our models to a dedicated test set taken from a larger set of subtitles from public broadcasts with audio in Finnish, Swedish or English. For this, intralingual subtitles (subtitles in the language of the original audio) are aligned with interlingual subtitles of the same programme in another language. The test set was carefully checked and non-corresponding segments are removed. Note that interlingual subtitles are produced independently from intralingual ones and, therefore, do not refer to direct translations of one another. Subtitles for the hard-of-hearing are also included but in a separate subset.

benchmark	sentence-level		document-level	
	BLEU	**chrF$_2$**	**BLEU**	**chrF$_2$**
fi→sv	18.8	0.443	19.3	0.451
sv→fi	15.7	0.449	16.8	0.462
fi→en	21.5	0.458	23.6	0.472
en→fi	16.0	0.444	17.1	0.454

Table 1: Comparison of BLEU and chrF$_2$ scores on the benchmark test set for the sentence-level and document-level systems in the language pairs Finnish→Swedish, Swedish→Finnish, Finnish→English, and English→Finnish.

Translation results for different subsets (scores calculated for spans of all subtitles within a video) are listed in Table 1. Evaluation of document-level translation required one additional step of aligning the automatically generated translations with corresponding reference translations. For this, we apply standard sentence alignment algorithms implemented in hunalign (Varga et al., 2005) using the re-alignment flag to enable lexical matching that ought to be very beneficial in this monolingual alignment task. Note that the automatic alignment may have negative effects on the final BLEU scores further supporting the strong result achieved by the document-level models compared to sentence-level ones according to the automatic evaluation. The scores indicate a consistent gain in using document-level information in both language pairs and all translation directions. Later, in Section 5, we will see, however, that the encouraging result does not hold in the manual assessment, which is most probably due to problems in segmentation and time frame alignment that we will discuss in the section below.

3.2 Subtitle frame alignment

One of the crucial steps in subtitle translation is the assignment to appropriate time slots. Our approach is to map translations back into the frames defined in the original source language subtitles assuming that they can fit in a similar way as the source language text was segmented. Those subtitle frames may include multiple sentences and sentences may stretch over several frames. Sentence extraction from the original subtitles is done with the techniques proposed by Tiedemann (2008). Time allocation of the translated sentences is implemented as yet another alignment algorithm.

Subtitles converted to sentence-level segments in XML:

```
<s id="13">
  <time id="T16S" value="00:01:05,960" />
We have to make readmission agreements with
other countries, -
  <time id="T16E" value="00:01:12,360" />
  <time id="T17S" value="00:01:12,440" />
so that they would be willing.
 </s>
  <s id="14">
We have to cooperate closely.
  <time id="T17E" value="00:01:17,440" />
 </s>
```

Mapped back to subtitle frames after translation:

```
16
00:01:05,960 --> 00:01:12,360
Meidän on tehtävä
takaisinottosopimuksia muiden maiden kanssa,

17
00:01:12,440 --> 00:01:17,440
jotta ne olisivat halukkaita.
Meidän on tehtävä tiivistä yhteistyötä.
```

Figure 1: Pre- and post-processing of subtitle data before and after translation. Sentences may run over several subtitle frames and multiple sentences and sentence fragments can also appear in the same time frame. The translation comes from a document-level model.

Once again, we apply a length-based sentence alignment model to map translations to the given time slots in the source language frames. In contrast to standard bitext alignment we are now interested in 1-to-n alignments only in which each existing subtitle frame needs to be filled with one or more segments coming from the automatically generated translations. For the target language segmentation we consider simple heuristics for splitting sentences into clauses by breaking strings that are separated by punctuation plus space characters. Resulting sequences that exceed a certain length threshold are further split on space characters closest to the center of the string. After that, we apply the famous Gale & Church algorithm (Gale and Church, 1993) to optimise the global alignment between source segments (original subtitle frame data) and target segments with adjusted parameters referring to our specific task: (1) We apply a uniform prior over alignment types as there is no strong preference for frame-to-clause alignment in our case. (2) We define alignment types to include one-to-x units only with x ranging from one to four. (3) We introduce extra costs to discourage frame boundaries within running sentences and assignments that violate length constraints. Figure 1 shows an example outcome of the procedure.

Finally, we also apply simple heuristics to insert line breaks making them conform to length and formatting constraints. During the manual assessment, we found out that this segmentation and the introduction of length violation costs caused severe damage to the time slot assignment pointing out the importance of proper optimisations of those steps. The implementation of our frame alignment algorithm is available as an open source package.[3]

4 Subtitle post-editing experiment and collecting user feedback

The study described in this paper is a part of a research project involving MT and other technologies as a tool for managing and processing AV material. The purpose of this study was

---

[3] https://github.com/Helsinki-NLP/subalign

to investigate the usability of MT for interlingual subtitling in an experiment carried out in November–December 2019 with professional subtitle translators using MT and PE to subtitle short video clips. The experiment involved recording process data with keylogging software (Inputlog, see Leijten and Van Waes, 2013). The translators' subjective evaluations of the usability of MTPE for subtitling were collected with a questionnaire focused on the user experience and semi-structured interviews. In this paper, we focus on these subjective evaluations and the professional translators' user experience of MT and PE for subtitling.

4.1 Participants and the subtitling workflow context

The experiments were carried out at the Finnish public broadcasting company Yle which produces and broadcasts AV content on television and an online streaming service. The company employs in-house translators and outsources some translation work. Subtitling is the most common approach to AVT in this company and Finland in general. Subtitle templates are generally not used by Yle, rather, the translators' normal workflow involves first translation from audio and spotting the subtitles manually. The translators follow quality recommendations which specify, for example, technical recommendations like number of characters in subtitle frames, minimum and maximum duration of subtitle frames on screen and maximum reading speed, as well as linguistic features. National guidelines for subtitle translation published in 2020[4] reflect the practices already in place at the broadcasting company.

The subtitling tasks were carried out in four language pairs: Finnish→Swedish, Swedish→Finnish, Finnish→English and English→Finnish. Twelve translators (three per language pair) participated in the experiment: eight in-house translators and four freelancers with between 4 and 30 years of professional experience as subtitle translators in the relevant language pair. Two participants stated they had experimented with using MT for subtitling prior to this test, and seven others had used MT for other purposes.

4.2 Materials and subtitling tasks

Video clips to be subtitled were selected from datasets representing two content types: EU election debates (unscripted dialogue between multiple participants) and lifestyle or cultural programmes (semi-scripted dialogue or monologue by programme hosts on various topics e.g. movies, food and drink). Each clip was selected so that it (1) formed a coherent, self-contained section of the program as a whole; (2) was approximately 3 minutes long; and (3) contained approximately 30–35 intralingual subtitles. The length and number of clips was limited due to the limited availability of participants for the experiments. Some clips consisted of complete programmes of suitable length, while others were cut from longer programmes ensuring that they formed a coherent, self-contained section. Human-generated intralingual subtitles in the source language were translated with two different MT models, and aligned to SRT files using the subtitle segmentation and timing from the intralingual subtitles as detailed in Section 3.1.

The subtitling tasks were carried out using the subtitlers' preferred subtitling software (Wincaps Q4 or Spot). An external monitor and keyboard were provided, and the subtitlers had access to the internet as well as terminology and other resources normally used in their work. The participants were instructed to create subtitles that would be acceptable for broadcasting, and to follow their normal working processes, but to not spend excessive time on "polishing" any given wording or on researching information. No explicit time limit was given, rather, the participants were instructed to work at their own pace.

Each participant carried out six tasks: MTPE for four clips (two clips with sentence-level MT output and two clips with document-level MT output), and translation from scratch for two clips, with spoken audio as source and manual spotting. To mitigate potential differences related

---

[4]Currently available in Finnish and Swedish: `http://www.av-kaantajat.fi/Laatusuositukset/`.

to difficulty of each clip and facilitation effect, the clips and MT outputs were rotated so that each clip was subtitled with no MT output, with sentence-level MT output and with document-level MT output by a different participant, and task order was varied. An experimenter was present to set up each task, assist with any potential technical issues and conduct the post-task interview, but did not interact with the participants during the tasks.

4.3 User Experience Questionnaire

An online form was used to collect subjective evaluations of the usability of the MT output for PE. The questionnaire was based on the User Experience Questionnaire (UEQ) developed by Laugwitz et al. (2008) for end-user evaluation of software products. The objective of the UEQ is to provide users with a "simple and immediate way to express feelings, impressions and attitudes" toward the product and thereby elicit quick but comprehensive assessments of user experience (Laugwitz et al., 2008, 64). It consists of scalar ratings of opposing adjective pairs (e.g. *practical/impractical*) intended to measure both classic usability aspects and user experience aspects. The adjective pairs are shown on an scale of 1–7, with positive and negative adjectives alternating on the left/right.

Because the focus of our study was on the participants' experience of MTPE rather than subtitling software, a modified version of the UEQ was created to focus on the participant's experience of PE as a process. Adjective pairs focusing on the attractiveness or usability of the software interface were omitted, and some adjective pairs were added to elicit responses more focused on PE. The final questionnaire was provided to the participants in Finnish, and contained the following 13 adjective pairs[5], preceded by the words *Post-editing was...: difficult/easy, unpleasant/pleasant, stressful/relaxed, labourious/effortless, slow/fast, inefficient/efficient, boring/exciting, tedious/fun, complicated/simple, annoying/enjoyable, limiting/creative, demotivating/motivating, impractical/practical.* For analysis, we processed the scores using the formulae in the UEQ Data Analysis Tools (version 7)[6] to convert them to a scale of -3 to +3, with 0 representing a neutral mid-point. In the UEQ Data Analysis Tool, average scores between -0.8 and +0.8 are defined as neutral evaluations. Values below -0.8 correspond to negative and values above 0.8 to positive evaluations.

In addition to the PE experience, we included Likert-scale assessments for the automatic spotting and segmentation of subtitle frames (1 poor – 7 good) and the effort needed to correct them (1 easy – 7 a lot of effort). Short open questions were included for more specific comments regarding the MT output, subtitle spotting and segmentation.

4.4 Semi-structured interviews

After completing all PE tasks, a brief semi-structured interview was also carried out to collect more detailed feedback on each participant's experience, features affecting the process and usability, and possible suggestions for future development and improvements. In the interview, the participants were first asked for their overall impression of the PE tasks was, what features of the MT output affected that impression experience and whether they observed differences between the outputs. They were then asked to describe their normal subtitling process and how the MT output affected that process. Finally, the participants were asked whether they would consider using MT as a tool in their own work and what kind of improvements would be needed.

The interviews were transcribed and anonymised, and thematic analysis (see e.g. Matthews and Ross, 2010) was carried out using the analysis software Atlas.ti. The interview responses were analysed for positive and negative comments and specific issues raised by the participants,

---

[5]The Finnish translations provided in version 8 of UEQ were not yet available at the time of our experiment. The Finnish adjective pairs were created by the authors, and we provide here our back-translations into English.

[6]https://www.ueq-online.org/

such as features impacting quality and usability or suggestions for improvement. In some cases, the participant's statement was not explicitly positive or negative, but rather consisted of a neutral, generic observation or a mixed evaluation, such as a comment (sv-fi, participant A) that the MT was "sometimes surprisingly good but sometimes surprisingly bad". Such cases were labelled as mixed/neutral.

5   Results

5.1   Evaluations of User Experience

Figure 2 shows the UEQ scores for each adjective pair averaged over all participants and all clips in each language pair comparing the two MT outputs (sentence-level model and document-level model). On average, the participants appeared to describe their MTPE experience in neutral terms (values between -0.8 and +0.8). Averaged across all participants, the most negative reactions were seen for *labourious/effortless* and *limiting/creative*, although these did not cross the -0.8 threshold. No clear differences emerged between the two different MT outputs, although the participants appeared to have a slight preference for the sentence-level MT output. Similarly, no clear difference was observed for the two programme types. Overall scores for lifestyle/cultural clips were slightly higher, except in Swedish→Finnish, where the election debate clips received slightly higher scores.

Interestingly, the participants' experiences appeared to differ in different language pairs. In particular, the participants working with English→Finnish evaluated nearly all adjective pairs negatively; only *stressful/relaxed* and *complicated/simple* show neutral averages in this language pair. Responses for Swedish→Finnish were more neutral, although tending toward negative. For Finnish→Swedish, evaluations were generally neutral, except *difficult/easy* and *complicated/simple*, where averages for the document-level output crossed the 0.8 threshold to positive evaluation. Finally, for Finnish→English clearly negative scores were seen only for the adjective pair *limiting/creative*, and the sentence-level output reaches positive averages for *difficult/easy*, *stressful/relaxed*, *inefficient/efficient*, *complicated/simple* and *demotivating/motivating*.

Spotting and segmentation of subtitle frames was generally assessed as poor, and problems appeared to have been more common in the document-level output. Correcting spotting and segmentation, however, was mostly characterised as neutral or easy. The participants working with English→Finnish assessed spotting/segmentation as particularly poor and difficult to correct, which may have affected their general impression of the PE process as a whole.

5.2   Analysis of positive and negative statements in user interviews

Table 2 shows the numbers of positive, negative and mixed/neutral statements identified. Of the total 143 statements, 55% (79) were classified as negative. Positive statements accounted for 29% (42) and mixed/neutral statements for 15% (22). No differences were observed between the two MT outputs. most statements characterised MT in general without reference to specific output. In cases where a specific output was identifiable, the numbers of positive, negative and mixed statements were roughly equal between the two outputs. However, some differences can be seen between language pairs. The proportion of negative statements is higher in Swedish→Finnish and English→Finnish than in the other two language pairs. Finnish→English translators have the highest number of positive statements, and Finnish→Swedish translators the highest proportion of mixed/neutral statements.

A more detailed analysis was also conducted to identify the specific issue discussed in negative and positive statements. Most common issues involved spotting/segmentation of the subtitles, MT output quality, and the effect of MT and PE on the translator's workflow and processes. Some statements also concerned other issues like the clips and their subject matter.

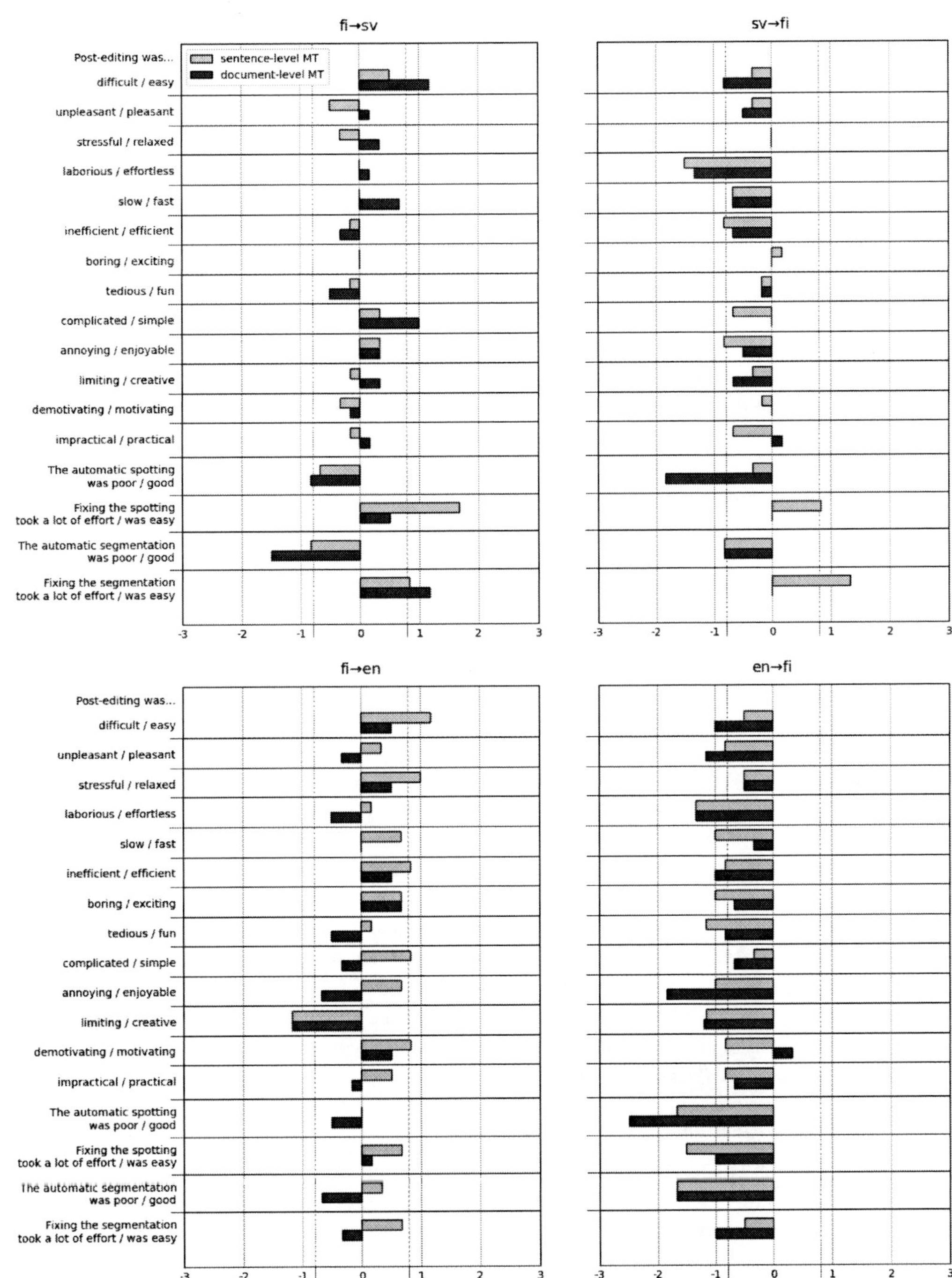

Figure 2: Average user experience scores comparing post-editing of sentence-level and document-level MT output in the language pairs Finnish→Swedish, Swedish→Finnish, Finnish→English and English→Finnish. Dashed lines represent the range [-0.8, +0.8], defined as neutral evaluations in the UEQ Data Analysis Tool.

Statement type	en→fi	fi→en	fi→sv	sv→fi	Total
Positive	13	16	8	5	42
Negative	23	19	14	23	79
Mixed/neutral	2	3	10	7	22
Total	38	38	32	35	143

Table 2: Positive, negative and mixed/neutral statements in the translator interviews

Most negative statements (33 out of 79) concerned the spotting or segmentation of subtitle frames, which all 12 participants commented on negatively. Specific problems involved subtitles being out of sync with the audio, and cases where a sentence had been incorrectly split into two (or more) segments. Two participants felt that the MT output tried to pack "too much" into a subtitle frame and that the machine was not able to condense the translation. Although the translations were created based on intralingual subtitles, which often already involve some condensation compared to the audio, this may suggest further differences between source and target languages. Three statements regarding the spotting were mixed/neutral, and the only two positive statements qualified spotting as "better" in some clips.

MT output quality received 30 negative mentions. Specific issues included lexical errors like mistranslated words or "odd" word choices (8 statements) and accuracy errors involving longer passages (5 statements), as well as fluency issues like ungrammatical or unidiomatic structures (6 statements). Two participants also noted omissions (words or longer passages) in the MT output. The remaining negative statements referred to MT output in general, without naming specific issues. On the other hand, the participants made 23 positive statements concerning MT quality. Specific comments referred to useful terminology and other lexical choices (9 statements) and fluency of the output (3 statements), while 11 positive statements involved general characterisations of the output as good or useful. Additionally, 13 mixed/neutral statements were made involving MT output quality in general terms.

The effect of MT and PE on the subtitling process was mentioned in 42 statements, which were mostly negative. In 15 statements, the participants commented that using MT and PE seemed to involve more effort than translation from scratch and to reduce productivity. A positive effect on productivity was mentioned in 3 statements, and 9 statements characterised the effect as mixed, sometimes reducing but sometimes increasing effort. Negative comments regarding effects also included an impression of being limited by the MT (8 statements) and potentially lower quality of the final translation (5 statements). Finally, 12 statements were made characterising the overall PE experience positively, while 5 statements described the experience negatively, and 8 in mixed/neutral terms.

5.3 User feedback for improvements

In total 28 suggestions involving development and improvement were identified in the transcripts. The most commonly mentioned improvement need was spotting/segmentation of the subtitles (8 statements). Two participants mentioned segmentation according to speaker changes as particularly useful. On the other hand, two participants would have preferred to see the MT output separately without segmentation, and one wished to see automatic speech recognition output of the original audio. Other specific issues mentioned involved need for condensing the MT output for subtitles (2 statements), improving cohesion, genre adaptation and punctuation in subtitles. Two participants mentioned the multimodal nature of AVT, one remarking that the machine is not able to take the visual aspect into account and the other wondering whether MT could use visual information.

Integration of functionalities other than MT into the subtitling software was also mentioned by some participants. Some type of terminology tool integration was mentioned in 4 statements. Some wished for a tool like a translation memory (4 statements), where one or more translators could add their own material and see how things were translated previously.

Of the participants, four would consider using MT for subtitling, although all would like to see some improvements in quality, while two participants stated they could not see themselves using MT as a tool at all. The other six gave a more mixed answer, stating that they could see MT and PE suitable for some situations but not others, for example, depending on the type of programme and subject matter. Some considered MT most useful for unfamiliar content as a terminology aid. In contrast, others would only use MT with subject matter they were already familiar with, to make sure to notice possible errors. With regard to genre, some stated MT seemed more useful for the election debates, with more formal speech, while others considered it more suitable for "simpler", less formal language in some of the lifestyle clips.

6 Discussion and ongoing work

The subjective evaluations offer valuable insight into the user experience of MTPE for subtitling. Our participants did not find PE particularly difficult or complicated, but they tended to characterise it negatively as limiting and annoying in the questionnaire, and these themes are further present in the interviews. The translators' feelings of MT limiting their creativity are similar to findings in studies addressing literary translation (Moorkens et al., 2018) as well as localisation (Guerberof Arenas, 2013). Translators in other studies have similarly referred to being "trapped by MT" (Bundgaard, 2017) and expressed concerns of a detrimental effect on the quality of the final translation (Moorkens et al., 2018; Matusov et al., 2019).

Both the questionnaire and the interviews point to problems in the MT subtitle alignment. Although the frame alignment (see Section 3.2) produces subtitles conforming to technical length constraints, the translators did not always find *way* the content was segmented acceptable. In some files, omissions or repetition of content in the MT also caused misalignments. The overall assessment of user experience also appears more negative in the language pairs where the participants rated the timing and segmentation poorest. This suggests that alignment problems may have affected the overall experience in addition to the MT output quality. One participant explicitly stated that dealing with off-sync subtitles probably led them to make also linguistic changes that may have been unnecessary.

In the interviews, most participants did not think MTPE increased productivity, some even felt the opposite. Similar observations have again been made in other studies; Etchegoyhen et al. (2014), for example, discuss how the increased cognitive load of dealing with MT output is a significant part of productivity. Although a detailed discussion of the process data is not within the scope of this paper, some parallels can be seen in our productivity measurements. On average, task times for MTPE were slightly faster than for translation from scratch, although considerable variation was observed between different files and participants. Five out of twelve participants were in fact slower when post-editing, concurring with the translators' mixed experience. For a more detailed analysis of the productivity metrics, see Koponen et al. (2020).

Some care is needed when interpreting the results. Firstly, it is important to note that the participants in this study did not have prior experience with MT for subtitling (only two had previously tested it). Their responses may therefore be affected by the unfamiliarity of the task, which some participants mentioned in the interviews (see also similar observations by Bywood et al., 2017). Secondly, the participants are used to doing first translation from audio instead of working with subtitle templates. Since the MT outputs were created using intralingual subtitles as the source text, rather than the spoken language, the participants may additionally have been affected by the intralingual subtitler's choices regarding spotting, paraphrasing and condensation. These may then have been perceived as issues in the MT output, such as omissions. More detailed communication regarding how the subtitles had been automatically generated could have clarified this issue for the participants. Finally, to allow the participants to follow their normal subtitling processes, they used their preferred subtitling software in the PE tasks. However, these tools (and AVT tools in general) are not designed for MTPE, and may therefore not be optimal for the task. This may also have affected the participants' perception of PE, and exploring AVT tools with more effective support for MTPE would be needed.

In view of our observations, it is clear that more work is needed to address the issues pointed out by the participants. It seems relevant to also compare experiences in a contrastive MTPE setting based on automatic AV transcriptions, in order to neutralise creative constraints imposed by subtitling choices carried over from intralingual subtitles. Following the interviews, we have made an effort to improve our MT pipeline in response to the segmentation and time frame alignment issues, and added support for machine-generated transcripts and time frames via automatic speech recognition and spotting. We have fixed some errors in our segmentation procedure for subtitle translations, and updated our heuristics to be less strict in enforcing length limits and clause breaks. Currently, our pipeline also makes use of an additional *restoration* stage as an endcap for MT pre-processing, implemented in practice as "intralingual translation" going from case- and punctuation-stripped input to fully-formatted output within the same language. The goal of this stage is to boost translation performance on automatic transcripts (where the MT is sensitive to differences in input formatting), and also of segmentation heuristics for post-processing (which are heavily dependent on punctuation in determining clause boundaries). Improvements to the MT and segmentation have been evaluated in further MTPE user tests during summer/fall 2020 with most of the same participants, and analysis of the data is still underway. Preliminary observations suggest somewhat more positive views of MT quality and segmentation, but the use of automatic transcriptions was received more negatively.

7   Conclusion

In this paper, we have presented a user evaluation of MTPE for subtitle translation based on experiments carried out by twelve professional subtitle translators in four language pairs (Finnish↔Swedish and Finnish↔English). Our analysis of data collected with a user experience questionnaire showed that, on average, translators' impression of MTPE varied from negative to neutral or mildly positive depending on language pair. Thematic analysis of interviews provided further information of the translators' experience. While translators did not consider PE particularly difficult, they tended to characterise it as limiting and somewhat annoying. Most, however, were open to using MT for at least some subtitling content. Further work on the quality of the outputs and tools is needed, and the translators' feedback provided valuable insight for this work. In both the questionnaire and interviews, the segmentation and timing of MT subtitles were identified as major issues, in addition to overall MT quality. As this paper reports our first user evaluations of MT for subtitling in specific language pairs and in a specific AVT context, definitive conclusions regarding the ultimate applicability of MTPE for subtitling naturally cannot yet be made. As work in this area continues, further studies on the user experience of subtitle translators are essential to investigate this question.

Acknowledgements

This work is part of the MeMAD project, funded by the European Union's Horizon 2020 Research and Innovation Programme (Grant Agreement No 780069).

References

Bundgaard, K. (2017). Translator attitudes towards translator-computer interaction - Findings from a workplace study. *Hermes– Journal of Language and Communication in Business*, 56:125–144.

Bywood, L., Georgakopoulou, P., and Etchegoyhen, T. (2017). Embracing the threat: machine translation as a solution for subtitling. *Perspectives: Studies in Translatology*, 25(3):492–508.

de Sousa, S. C., Aziz, W., and Specia, L. (2011). Assessing the post-editing effort for automatic and semi-automatic translations of DVD subtitles. In *Proceedings of RANLP 2011*, pages 97–103.

Etchegoyhen, T., Bywood, L., Fishel, M., Georgakopoulou, P., Jiang, J., Van Loenhout, G., Del Pozo, A., Maučec, M. S., Turner, A., and Volk, M. (2014). Machine translation for subtitling: A large-scale evaluation. In *Proceedings of the 9th International Conference on Language Resources and Evaluation, LREC 2014*, pages 46–53.

Gale, W. A. and Church, K. W. (1993). A program for aligning sentences in bilingual corpora. *Computational Linguistics*, 19(1):75–102.

Guerberof Arenas, A. (2013). What do professional translators think about post-editing. *The Journal of Specialised Translation*, 19(19):75–95.

Junczys-Dowmunt, M. (2019). Microsoft Translator at WMT 2019: Towards large-scale document-level neural machine translation. In *Proceedings of the Fourth Conference on Machine Translation*, pages 225–233.

Junczys-Dowmunt, M., Grundkiewicz, R., Dwojak, T., Hoang, H., Heafield, K., Neckermann, T., Seide, F., Germann, U., Aji, A. F., Bogoychev, N., Martins, A. F. T., and Birch, A. (2018). Marian: Fast neural machine translation in C++. In *Proceedings of ACL 2018, System Demonstrations*, pages 116–121.

Karakanta, A., Negri, M., and Turchi, M. (2020a). Is 42 the answer to everything in subtitling-oriented speech translation? In *Proceedings of the 17th International Conference on Spoken Language Translation*, pages 209–219, Online. Association for Computational Linguistics.

Karakanta, A., Negri, M., and Turchi, M. (2020b). MuST-cinema: a speech-to-subtitles corpus. In *Proceedings of The 12th Language Resources and Evaluation Conference*, pages 3727–3734, Marseille, France. European Language Resources Association.

Koponen, M., Sulubacak, U., Vitikainen, K., and Tiedemann, J. (2020). MT for subtitling: User evaluation of post-editing productivity. In *Proceedings of the 22nd Annual Conference of the European Association for Machine Translation*, pages 115–124, Lisboa, Portugal. European Association for Machine Translation.

Kudo, T. and Richardson, J. (2018). SentencePiece: A simple and language independent subword tokenizer and detokenizer for neural text processing. In *Proceedings of the 2018 EMNLP*, pages 66–71.

Laugwitz, B., Held, T., and Schrepp, M. (2008). Construction and evaluation of a user experience questionnaire. In Holzinger, A., editor, *HCI and Usability for Education and Work. USAB 2008*, volume 5298 of *Lecture Notes in Computer Science*, pages 63–76, Berlin/Heidelberg. Springer.

Leijten, M. and Van Waes, L. (2013). Keystroke logging in writing research: Using Inputlog to analyze and visualize writing processes. *Written Communication*, 30(3):358–392.

Matthews, B. and Ross, L. (2010). *Research Methods: A Practical Guide for the Social Sciences*. Pearson Education Ltd, Edinburgh.

Matusov, E., Wilken, P., and Georgakopoulou, Y. (2019). Customizing neural machine translation for subtitling. In *Proceedings of the Fourth Conference on Machine Translation*, pages 82–93.

Melero, M., Oliver, A., and Badia, T. (2006). Automatic multilingual subtitling in the eTITLE project. In *Proceedings of Translating and the Computer 28*, pages 1–18.

Moorkens, J., Toral, A., Castilho, S., and Way, A. (2018). Translators' perceptions of literary post-editing using statistical and neural machine translation. *Translation Spaces*, 7(2):240–262.

Nikolić, K. (2015). The pros and cons of using templates in subtitling. In *Audiovisual Translation in a Global Context: Mapping an Ever-Changing Landscape*, pages 192–202.

Pedersen, J. (2017). The FAR model: assessing quality in interlingual subtitling. *The Journal of Specialised Translation*, 28:210–229.

Tiedemann, J. (2008). Synchronizing translated movie subtitles. In *Proceedings of LREC'08*.

Tiedemann, J. and Scherrer, Y. (2017). Neural machine translation with extended context. In *Proceedings of the Third DiscoMT*, pages 82–92.

Varga, D., Németh, L., Halácsy, P., Kornai, A., Trón, V., and Nagy, V. (2005). Parallel corpora for medium density languages. In *Proceedings of RANLP 2005*, pages 590–596.

Vaswani, A., Shazeer, N., Parmar, N., Uszkoreit, J., Jones, L., Gomez, A. N., Kaiser, Ł., and Polosukhin, I. (2017). Attention is all you need. In *Advances in Neural Information Processing Systems 30*, pages 5998–6008.

Volk, M., Sennrich, R., Hardmeier, C., and Tidström, F. (2010). Machine translation of TV subtitles for large scale production. In *Proceedings of the Second Joint EM+/CNGL Workshop*, pages 53–62.

Improving the Multi-Modal Post-Editing (MMPE) CAT Environment based on Professional Translators' Feedback

Nico Herbig[1]
Santanu Pal[2]
Tim Düwel[1]
Raksha Shenoy[1,3]
Antonio Krüger[1]
Josef van Genabith[1,3]

nico.herbig@dfki.de
santanu.pal2@wipro.com
tim.duewel@dfki.de
raksha.shenoy@dfki.de
antonio.krueger@dfki.de
josef.vangenabith@uni-saarland.de

[1]German Research Center for Artificial Intelligence (DFKI), Saarland Informatics Campus, Germany

[2]Wipro AI, Bangalore, India

[3]Department of Language Science and Technology, Saarland University, Germany

Abstract

More and more professional translators are switching to the use of post-editing (PE) to increase productivity and reduce errors. Even though PE requires significantly less text production, current computer-aided translation (CAT) interfaces still heavily focus on traditional mouse and keyboard input and ignore other interaction modalities to support PE operations. Recently, a multi-modal post-editing (MMPE) CAT environment combining pen, touch, speech, multi-modal interaction, and conventional mouse and keyboard input possibilities was presented. The design and development of the first version of MMPE were informed by extensive consultation with professional translators. This paper details how MMPE was since further refined by professional translators' judgments on which interaction modalities are most suitable for which PE task and more general qualitative findings. In particular, we describe how the layout was adapted to avoid confusion, which visualization aids were added, how the handwriting input was improved, and how we enabled multi-word reordering through touch drag and drop, as well as how the speech and multi-modal interaction components were enhanced. Finally, we present a sneak preview of how we integrated eye tracking not only for logging but also as an input modality that can be used in combination with keyboard or speech commands.

1 Introduction

Due to significant improvements in machine translation (MT) quality over the past years,[1] more and more professional translators are integrating this technology into their translation workflows (Zaretskaya et al., 2016; Zaretskaya and Seghiri, 2018). The process of using a pre-translated but potentially erroneous text, often MT output, and improving it to create the final translation is called post-editing (PE). Translators' perceptions regarding post-editing range

---

[1]WMT translation task: `http://matrix.statmt.org/matrix` for newstest2019, accessed 23/07/2020

from strong dislikes in older research (Lagoudaki, 2009; Wallis, 2006), to questioning its benefit and being cautious about PE (Gaspari et al., 2014; Koponen, 2012), to seeing it as a threat to their profession (Moorkens, 2018). However, many users have dated perceptions of MT and often prefer PE over translating from scratch when confronted with modern MT (Green et al., 2013). Furthermore, perceptions regarding PE of experienced translators appear more negative (Moorkens and O'Brien, 2015) than those of novice translators (Yamada, 2015).

Even though translators remain critical regarding PE, productivity gains of 36% when using modern neural MT for PE (Toral et al., 2018) have been shown. Since the task changes from mostly text production to comparing and adapting MT and translation memory (TM) proposals, a thorough re-investigation of interface designs is required. For this, Herbig et al. (2019a) conducted an elicitation study to explore which interaction modalities could well support the PE process and found that translators envision PE interfaces relying on touch, pen, and speech input combined with mouse and keyboard as particularly useful. Initial tests by Teixeira et al. (2019) using touch for reordering and speech dictation further showed promising practical results. The recently presented MMPE prototype (Herbig et al., 2020c) combines even more modalities, namely standard mouse & keyboard input with touch, pen, and speech interactions for PE of MT, and their study shows that translators are enthusiastic about having these interaction possibilities. For deletions and reorderings, pen and touch modalities received good feedback and were efficient, while for insertions and replacements, speech and multi-modal input were perceived positively.

Apart from these main results, Herbig et al. (2020b) also presented a variety of qualitative findings. Here, we leverage this feedback to extend and improve the original MMPE CAT environment through a variety of layout changes, enhanced interaction flexibility, and others, as discussed below. Furthermore, we present a first glimpse of how we include eye tracking combined with speech or keyboard input as an additional interaction modality.

2 Related Work

This section presents related research on translation environments and pays special attention to interaction modalities other than mouse and keyboard.

2.1 CAT and Post-Editing

So-called CAT (computer-aided translation) environments offer features like MT and TM (translation memory) together with quality estimation and concordance functionality (Federico et al., 2014), alignments between source and MT (Schwartz et al., 2015), interactive MT offering assistance such as auto-completion (Green et al., 2014b,a), or intelligibility assessments (Coppers et al., 2018; Vandeghinste et al., 2016, 2019). Due to this feature-richness, most professional translators use CAT tools daily (van den Bergh et al., 2015).

Even though TM is still often valued higher than MT (Moorkens and O'Brien, 2017), in an experiment Vela et al. (2019) showed that professional translators choose MT in 80% of the cases when confronted with the choice between translation from scratch, TM, and MT, thus highlighting the importance of PE MT output. In terms of time savings, Zampieri and Vela (2014) find that PE is on average 28% faster for technical translations, Aranberri et al. (2014) show translation throughput is increased for both professionals and lay users when they do PE, and Läubli et al. (2013) find that PE also increases productivity in realistic environments. Apart from saving time, Green et al. (2013) showed that PE also reduces errors.

Obviously, the interaction pattern during PE changes in comparison to translation from scratch, leading to a significantly reduced amount of mouse and keyboard events (Carl et al., 2010; Green et al., 2013). Therefore, other modalities, in addition to mouse and keyboard, have been explored for PE, as we discuss in the next section.

2.2 Multi-Modal Approaches

Using automatic speech recognition has a long history for traditional translation from scratch (Dymetman et al., 1994; Brousseau et al., 1995), and dictating translations that are then manually transcribed by secretaries dates back even further (Theologitis, 1998). For PE, the more recent study of the SEECAT (Martinez et al., 2014) environment supporting automatic speech recognition (ASR) argues that its combination with typing could boost productivity. According to a survey by Mesa-Lao (2014), PE trainees have a positive attitude towards speech input and would consider adopting it, but only as a complement to other modalities. In a small-scale study, Zapata et al. (2017) found that ASR for PE was faster than ASR for translation from scratch. Nowadays, commercial CAT tools like memoQ and MateCat are also beginning to integrate ASR.

The CASMACAT tool (Alabau et al., 2013) further allows users to input text by handwriting with an e-pen in a separate area, where the handwriting is recognized and placed at the cursor position. A vision paper by Alabau and Casacuberta (2012) proposes to instead PE sentences with few errors by using copy-editing-like pen input directly on the text.

Studies on mobile PE via touch and speech within the Kanjingo app (O'Brien et al., 2014; Torres-Hostench et al., 2017) show that participants liked to drag and drop words for reordering. They further preferred speech input when translating from scratch, but used the iPhone keyboard for small modifications. Zapata (2016) also explores the use of speech and touch; however, the study did not focus on PE and used Microsoft Word instead of a proper CAT environment.

Teixeira et al. (2019) explore touch and speech in unaided translation, translation using TM, and translation using MT conditions. In their studies, touch input received poor feedback: Their visualization, having a tile per word that could be dragged and dropped, made reading more complicated, and touch insertions were rather complex in their implementation. In contrast, speech dictation was shown to be quite useful and even preferred to mouse and keyboard by half of the participants.

An elicitation study by Herbig et al. (2019a), exploring interaction modalities for PE in a structured way, indicates that pen, touch, and speech interaction should be combined with mouse and keyboard to improve PE of MT. Based on these findings, Herbig et al. (2020c,b) set out and built a prototype called MMPE. It combines mouse and keyboard input with pen, touch, and speech modalities: "Users can directly cross out or hand-write new text, drag and drop words for reordering, or use spoken commands to update the text in place" (Herbig et al., 2020c). Furthermore, their system focused on easily interpretable logs for translation process research that directly show whether users deleted, inserted, reordered, or replaced tokens during PE, thus improving on prior works' logs, which usually only show which keypresses occurred at which timestamps. Their study with professional translators suggested that "pen and touch interaction are suitable for deletion and reordering tasks, while they are of limited use for longer insertions. On the other hand, speech and multi-modal combinations of select & speech are considered suitable for replacements and insertions but offer less potential for deletion and reordering" (Herbig et al., 2020b).

In summary, previous research suggests that professional translators can increase productivity and reduce errors through PE; however, translators themselves are not always eager to switch to PE. It has been argued that the PE process might be better supported by using different modalities in addition to the conventional mouse and keyboard approaches, and a few prototypes showed promising results. The most diverse investigation of multi-modal interaction for PE by Herbig et al. (2020b) provided interesting insights into the modalities' advantages and disadvantages. However, the study also presented plenty of qualitative findings. Based on these, our work further improves and extends MMPE, as discussed in the next sections.

3 Improvements and Extensions to MMPE

This section presents the MMPE prototype and how we extended it. Overall, the prototype combines pen, touch, eye, and speech input with a traditional mouse and keyboard approach for PE of MT and focuses on professional translators in an office setting. We will introduce the full prototype and focus on how the original implementation (presented in Herbig et al. (2020c)) was extended and improved based on the feedback received from professional translators in Herbig et al. (2020b).

3.1 Hardware and Software Overview

The frontend is the key MMPE component to explore different interaction modalities, and was developed using Angular[2]. The backend, implemented using node.js[3], was kept rather minimal, only allowing saving and loading of projects from JSON files, and forwarding text/audio to spellchecking or audio transcription services. We continue to focus on the frontend, and only slightly extend the backend services where necessary.

To optimally support the developed interactions, Herbig et al. (2020c) proposed to use a large touch and pen screen that can be tilted (see Figure 1), specifically the Wacom Cintiq Pro 32 inch display with the Flex Arm. The tilting mechanism thereby aims to better support handwriting. While this setup is rather expensive (ca. 3500 Euro), the web-based application could be used on any cheaper touch and pen device, as the usage of Bootstrap[4] supports layouts on different resolutions. However, one should make sure that the display is large and reacts quickly to handwritten input.

Figure 1: Hardware setup with a large tiltable screen, a digital pen, mouse, keyboard, a headset, and an eye tracker.

Furthermore, a headset should be used for the prototype, as the transcription used for interpreting speech commands often yields bad results when using only internal microphones. The original study used a Sennheiser PC 8 here (ca. 35 Euro), but informal tests showed that most external microphones work well. A remote eye tracker (the Tobii 4C, ca. 200 Euro) is

---

[2]https://angular.io/, accessed 27/07/2020
[3]https://nodejs.org/en/, accessed 27/07/2020
[4]https://getbootstrap.com/, accessed 27/07/2020

attached to the screen and calibrated to the user with the provided eye tracking software, but
other eye trackers could of course also be integrated. Naturally, MMPE also allows input using
mouse and keyboard.

3.2   Overall Layout

Figure 2 shows our implemented horizontal source-target layout.   Each segment's status
(unedited, edited, confirmed) is visualized between source and target. On the far right, support tools are offered, as explained in Section 3.3. The top of the interface shows a toolbar
where users can save, load, and navigate between projects, and enable or disable spellchecking,
whitespace visualization, speech recognition, and eye tracking, which will be discussed below.

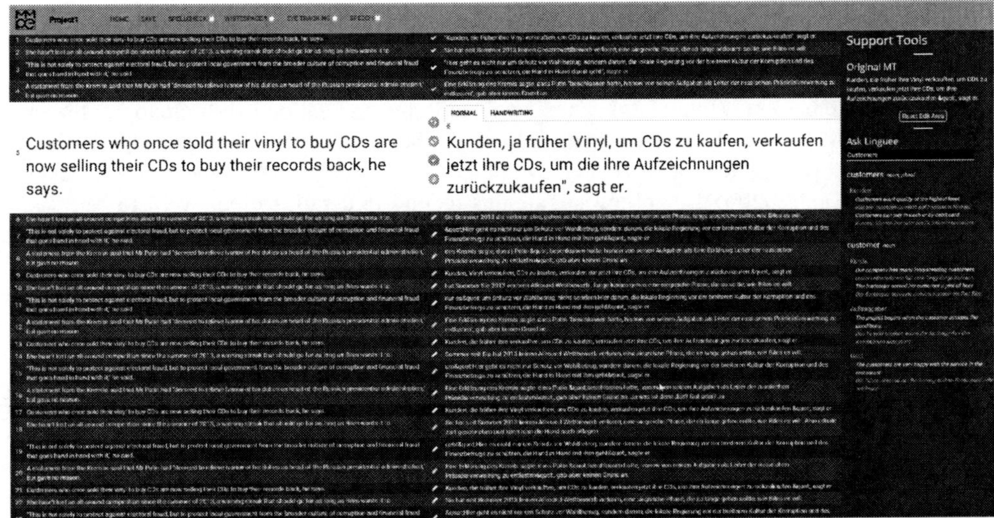

Figure 2: Screenshot of the interface.

The current segment is enlarged, thereby offering space for handwritten input and allowing
users to view the context while still seeing the current segment in a comfortable manner (as
requested in Herbig et al. (2019a)). The view for the current segment is further divided into
the source segment (left) and tabbed editing planes for the target (right), one for handwriting
and drawing gestures, and one for touch deletion & reordering, as well as standard mouse and
keyboard input. By clicking on the tabs at the top, the user can quickly switch between the two
modes. As the prototype focuses on PE, the target views initially show the MT proposal to be
edited. The reason for having two editing fields instead of only one is that some interactions are
overloaded, e.g., a touch drag can be interpreted as both hand-writing and reordering, depending
on the tab in which it is performed. Undo and redo functionality and segment confirmation are
also implemented: (1) By using hotkeys, (2) through buttons between source and target (next to
an additional button for touch deletions, see below), or (3) through speech commands.

We decided to stick with the enlarged visualization of the current segment, as participants
in Herbig et al. (2020b) liked the large font size. However, the original prototype had the
two target views (handwriting and default editing) next to each other. Thus, overall, three
neighboring views. This was perceived as unintuitive, leading to much confusion, especially
at the beginning of the experiment, when participants did not remember which target view
supported which features. Therefore, we combined the two, clearly labelling which mode does
what, and allowing switching between them using the tabs quickly. The combination has the

additional advantages that the interface becomes symmetric (as there is only one source and target for the previous, the current, and the remaining segments). Furthermore, the space for hand-writing increases even further, and the layout on smaller displays with insufficient space to nicely visualize three text boxes next to each other is improved.

Currently, we are adding further customization possibilities as requested by the participants in Herbig et al. (2020b), e.g., to adapt the font size or to switch between displaying source and target side by side or one above the other.

3.3 Support Tools and Visualization Aids

In the **support tools** (Figure 2 right), the user can reset the target text to the unedited MT output using a button. Furthermore, a bilingual concordancer is offered: When entering a word in the search box or clicking/touching a word in the source view on the left, the Linguee[5] website is queried to show the word in context and display its primary and alternative translations. Here, we are planning to integrate further features like Google direct answers.

Spellchecking (Figure 3a) can be enabled in the navigation bar at the top of the interface: For this, MMPE analyzes the target text using either the browser's integrated spellchecker, the node.js simple-spellchecker package[6], or the Microsoft Cognitive Services spellchecker. While Herbig et al. (2020b) did not investigate this feature in detail, we believe it to be essential for practical usage, since the unavailability of spellchecking was criticized in Teixeira et al. (2019).

A feature that we newly introduced into the prototype because it was requested in Herbig et al. (2020b) was the **visualization of whitespaces**, which can also be enabled in the navigation bar. Figure 3b shows the visualized spaces and line breaks, commonly known from, e.g., Microsoft Word.

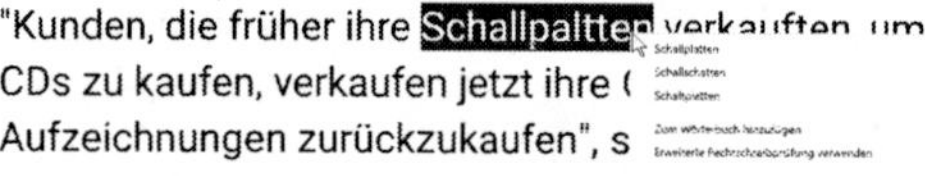

"Kunden, die·früher·ihre·Vinyl·verkauften,·um·CDs·zu·
kaufen,·verkaufen·jetzt·ihre·CDs,·um·ihre·
Aufzeichnungen·zurückzukaufen",·sagt·er.

<table>
<tr><td>(a) Spell checking.</td><td>(b) Visualization of whitespaces.</td></tr>
</table>

Figure 3: Spellchecking and whitespace visualization.

3.4 Hand-writing View

Hand-writing in the hand-writing tab (see Figure 4) is recognized using the MyScript Interactive Ink SDK[7], which worked well in Herbig et al. (2020b). The input field further offers drawing gestures[8] like strike-through or scribble for deletions, breaking a word into two (draw a line from top to bottom), and joining words (draw a line from bottom to top). If there is a lack of space to hand-write the intended text, the user can create such space by breaking the line (draw a long line from top to bottom). All changes are immediately applied, e.g., deleting a word by strike-through removes it immediately and does not show it in a struck-through visualization. A small button at the top right of the editor can be used to convert handwritten text into computer font; however, this is only for cosmetic reasons and not required for the functionality. The editor further shows the recognized input immediately at the top of the drawing view in a small gray font. Clicking on a word here offers alternatives that can be easily selected (see Figure 4).

---

[5]https://www.linguee.com/, accessed 27/07/2020

[6]https://www.npmjs.com/package/simple-spellchecker, accessed 27/07/2020

[7]https://developer.myscript.com/, accessed 27/07/2020

[8]https://developer.myscript.com/docs/concepts/editing-gestures/, accessed 27/07/2020

Apart from using the pen, the user can use his/her finger or the mouse for hand-writing. However, most participants in Herbig et al. (2020b) preferred the pen to finger hand-writing for insertions and replacements due to its precision, although some considered it less direct than finger input. One participant in the study even used the strike-through deletion with the mouse; therefore, we decided to keep all three hand-writing options.

In Herbig et al. (2020b), participants highly valued deletion by strike-through or scribbling through the text, as this would nicely resemble standard copy-editing. However, hand-writing for replacements and insertions was considered to work well only for short modifications. For more extended changes, participants argued that one should instead fall back to typing or speech commands. An issue that might have influenced this finding was that in the evaluated version of MMPE, an unintended change of the currently selected segment happened when the palm of the hand touched another piece of text. As it is common to lay down one's hand while writing, we now prevent this unintended segment change by ignoring palm touches.

Furthermore, participants found the gesture to create space (drawing a vertical line at the position) often hard to accomplish, which we improved by increasing the lineheight. For the first line, we added even more space to the top, to prevent a drawing from starting in the text box containing the recognized text, where it would be ignored, thereby improving the user experience. Last, we deactivated the button of the digital pen, as it frequently resulted in unintended right-clicks triggering the context menu.

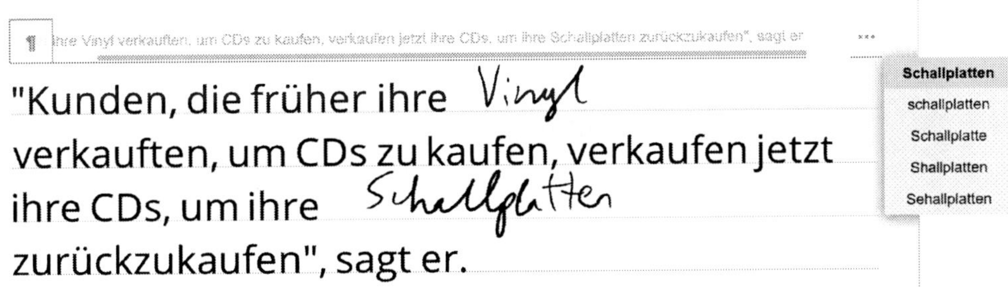

Figure 4: Hand-writing and alternatives after clicking the word "Schallplatten" in the recognized text at the top.

3.5 Default Editing View

Below we dive deeper into the interaction possibilities supported by the default editing view, and focus on improvements to these.

3.5.1 Mouse and Keyboard Input

Since mouse and keyboard inputs were still the fastest for insertion and replacement operations in the study by Herbig et al. (2020b), we naturally kept this feature, including the possibility of navigating using hotkeys like ctrl+arrow keys or copy & pasting using ctrl+c/v. Marking and drag and drop with the mouse are also supported as in any text processing application. However, since participants in the study stated that mouse and keyboard only work well due to years of experience and muscle memory, we will focus on other modalities in the remainder of this section.

3.5.2 Touch Reorder and Delete

Reordering using (pen or finger) touch is supported with a simple drag and drop procedure (see Figure 5b): For this, we visualize the picked-up word(s) below the touch position and show the calculated current drop position through a small arrow element. Spaces between words and punctuation marks are automatically fixed, i.e., double spaces at the pickup position are removed and missing spaces at the drop position are inserted. Furthermore, for the German language, nouns are automatically capitalized using the list of nouns from Wiktionary[9]. This reordering functionality is strongly related to Teixeira et al. (2019); however, only the currently dragged word is temporarily visualized as a tile to offer better readability.

Touch reordering was highlighted as particularly useful or even "perfect" as it "nicely resembles a standard correction task", and received the highest subjective scores and lowest time required for reordering (Herbig et al., 2020b). Nevertheless, the old reorder only supported moving one word at a time, not whole sub-phrases or parts of words, which is naturally needed in actual PE settings. Now, users have two options: (1) They can drag and drop single words by starting a drag directly on top of a word, or (2) they can double-tap to start a selection process, define which part of the sentence should be selected (e.g., multiple words or a part of a word, see Figure 5a), and then move it (see Figure 5b).

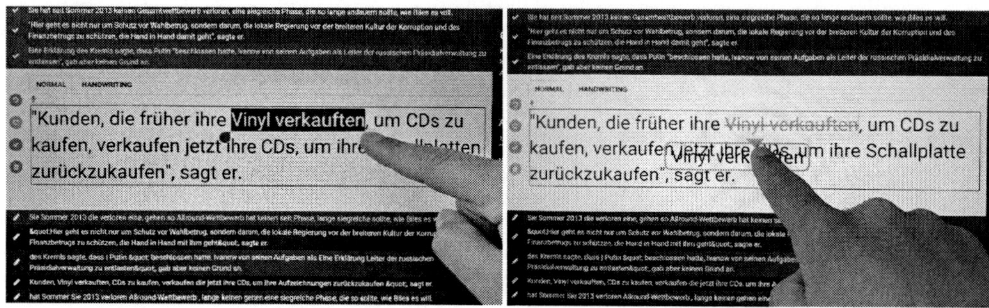

(a) Multi-word selection using touch. (b) Touch reorder.

Figure 5: Touch multi-word selection and reordering.

While this allows a much more flexible reorder functionality, it has the disadvantage that double-tap can no longer be used to delete words, as was the case in Herbig et al. (2020c). However, as strike-through in the hand-writing view was also highly liked for deletion, we think removing this functionality does not harm overall usability. Furthermore, we added a delete button alongside the undo/redo/confirm buttons so that users can still delete using touch by selecting text through double-tap and pressing the button then. Overall we believe that the increased flexibility should enhance usability, even though touch deletion of single words became slightly more complicated.

Several participants in Herbig et al. (2020b) noted that the text was jumping around when reordering a word from the end of a line: By immediately removing the picked-up word from the text, all remaining words moved to the front, and the placeholder element, was taking up space that also pushed words from line to line while dragging. We have now solved this issue by keeping the word(s) in the old position in a struck-through appearance (see Figure 5b), showing a copy of the word below the finger/pen, and only removing the actual word(s) on drop. Furthermore, the visualization was redesigned to make the drop position clearer without taking up any space, and highlighting the picked-up text better.

---

[9]`https://en.wiktionary.org/wiki/Category:German_noun_forms`, accessed 27/07/2020

3.6 Speech

To minimize lag during speech recognition, we use a streaming approach, sending the recorded audio to IBM Watson servers to receive a transcription, which is then interpreted in a command-based fashion. Thus, the speech module not only handles dictations as in Teixeira et al. (2019) but can correct mistakes in place. The transcription itself is shown at the top of the default editing view next to a microphone symbol (see Figure 6). As commands, post-editors can *"insert"*, *"delete"*, *"replace"*, and *"reorder"* words or sub-phrases. To specify the position if it is ambiguous, anchors can be specified, e.g., *"after"*/*"before"*/*"between"*, or the occurrence of the token (*"first"*/*"second"*/*"last"*) can be defined. A full example is *"replace A between B and C by D"*, where A, B, C, and D can be words or sub-phrases. Due to recognition and practicality issues, character-level speech commands are not supported, so instead of deleting an ending, one should replace the word, e.g., *"replace finding with find"* instead of *"delete i n g from finding"*. Again, spaces between words and punctuation marks are automatically fixed, and for German, nouns are capitalized as described for touch reordering.

In Herbig et al. (2020b), speech received good ratings for insertions and replacements, but worse ratings for reorderings and deletions. According to the participants, speech would become especially compelling for longer insertions and would be preferable when commands remain simple. However, it was considered problematic in shared offices and would be complex to formulate commands while mentally processing text. To limit the complexity of speech commands, we added further synonyms (e.g., *"write"* or *"put"* as alternatives to *"insert"*) and allow users to specify anchors by occurrence (e.g., *"delete last A"*). Thus, we increase flexibility and offer more natural commands that participants had used in Herbig et al. (2020b), but which were not supported back then. Furthermore, we now allow modifying punctuation marks (e.g., *"delete comma after nevertheless"*), automatically capitalize words inserted at the beginning, uncapitalize them when reordered to other positions, capitalize the second word when deleting the first in the sentence, and so on. Furthermore, users can now choose to restate the whole sentence when MT quality is low, and in general, we allow dictations.

We improved user feedback regarding speech commands: On the one hand, invalid commands display why they are invalid below the transcription (e.g., "Cannot delete comma after nevertheless, as nevertheless does not exist", or "There are multiple occurrences of nevertheless, please specify further"). On the other hand, it previously was hard to see if the speech module correctly interpreted the commanded change because the text was simply replaced. Thus, the interface now temporarily highlights insertions in green, deletions in red (the space at the position), and combinations of green and red for reordering and replacements, where the color fades away 0.5s after the command. That way, the user can quickly see if everything works as expected, or if further corrective commands are required, in which case a simple undo operation can be triggered (as before through the button, hotkey, or by simply saying *"undo"*).

(a) Target before speech command.

(b) Target after speech command with change highlighting.

Figure 6: Speech command.

Other ideas we are currently working on include passing the text to the speech recognition to improve transcription results by considering the context (Dymetman et al., 1994) or training the automatic speech recognition towards the user to improve the received transcription.

3.7 Multi-Modal Combination of Pen/Touch/Mouse with Speech

Multi-modal combinations of pen/touch/mouse combined with speech are also supported: Target word(s)/position(s) must first be specified by performing a text selection using the pen, finger touch, or the mouse/keyboard. Afterwards, the user can use a voice command like *"delete"*, *"insert A"*, *"move after/before A/between A and B"*, or *"replace with A"* without needing to specify the position/word, thereby making the commands less complex (see Figure 7).

" Kunden, die früher ihre Vinyl Schallplatten verkauften, um CDs zu kaufen, verkaufen jetzt ihre CDs, um ihre Aufzeichnungen zurückzukaufen", sagt er.

(a) Target before multi-modal command.

" Kunden, die früher ihre Vinyl verkauften, um CDs zu kaufen, verkaufen jetzt ihre CDs, um ihre Aufzeichnungen zurückzukaufen", sagt er.

(b) Target after multi-modal command with change highlighting.

Figure 7: Multi-modal command of selection and speech.

In Herbig et al. (2020b), multi-modal interaction received good ratings for insertions and replacements, but worse ratings for reorderings and deletions. One big issue for deletions and reorderings was that multi-word (or partial word) reorder/delete was not supported in the previous implementation; thus, the translator had to place the cursor followed by a speech command multiple times. Due to the possibility of touch selection of multiple (or partial) words, this is now possible using multi-modal combinations of pen/touch/mouse combined with simplified speech commands, thereby hopefully enhancing the user experience. We want to further offer the possibility to keep the selection more straightforward, i.e., allowing the user to place the cursor at one position, but then state, e.g., "delete two words". This should improve situations where speech-only commands are particularly complex due to ambiguities, in which the combined approach was highlighted as advantageous to the speech-only approach. Naturally, the other improvements for the speech case discussed above also work for the multi-modal case, thus hopefully making multi-modal interaction even more natural.

3.8 Eye Tracking

In Herbig et al. (2020b), insertions are the only operation where the multi-modal approach was (non-significantly) faster than speech-only commands, since the position did not have to be verbally specified. We therefore investigate other approaches to enhance the multi-modal case: Apart from improving it by supporting multi-word reorder/delete and simplifying the speech commands as discussed above, we are currently exploring the integration of an eye tracker. The idea is to simply fixate the word to be replaced/deleted/reordered or the gap used for insertion, and state the simplified speech command (e.g., *"replace with A"*/*"delete"*), instead of having to manually place the cursor through touch/pen/mouse/keyboard. Apart from possibly speeding up multi-modal interaction, this approach would also solve the issue reported by several participants in Herbig et al. (2020b) that one would have to "do two things at once", while keeping the advantage of having simple commands in comparison to the speech-only approach.

Our implementation currently only visualizes where the user looks: Upon activation in the Angular client's navigation bar, a request is sent to the node.js server, which launches a Python script for the communication with the eye tracker, and forwards the raw gaze events back to the client. The client can then detect fixations to tell the speech service the current gaze position so that it can be used for multi-modal commands. Figure 8 shows the recognized gaze position.

Apart from combining eye tracking with speech commands, we also plan to combine it with the keyboard, similar to the ReType approach (Sindhwani et al., 2019) but adapted towards the translation and in particular PE domain. Furthermore, we work on memorizing and visu-

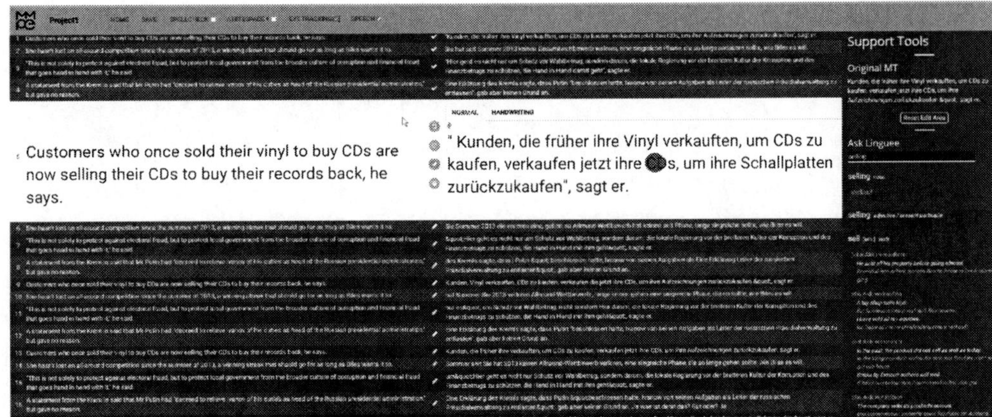

Figure 8: Eye tracking: User gazing at "CDs".

alizing the last fixation on the source and target views, thereby helping translators navigating through the text not to get lost when switching their attention back and forth between source and target. This approach is similar to GazeMarks (Kern et al., 2010), which has shown its efficiency in visual search tasks with attention shifts.

Our interface facilitates eye tracking, as the large font and screen also enable cheaper models like the Tobii 4C to have sufficient precision to detect words. However, we are currently integrating a more precise eye tracker to explore the differences for the application case.

3.9 Logging

MMPE supports extensive logging functionality: On the one hand, actual keystrokes, touched pixel coordinates, and other events are logged and all UI interactions (like *segmentChange* or *undo/redo/confirm*) are stored, allowing us to analyze the translator's use of MMPE.

Most importantly, however, we also log all text manipulations on a higher level to simplify text editing analysis. For *insertions*, we log whether a single or multiple words were inserted, and add the actual words and their positions as well as the segment's content before and after the insertion to the log entry. *Deletions* are logged analogously, and for *reorderings*, we save the old and the new position of the moved word(s) to the log entry. Last, for *replacements*, we log whether only a part of a word was replaced (i.e., changing the word form), whether the whole word was replaced (i.e., correcting the lexical choice), or whether a group of words was replaced. In all cases, the word(s) before and after the change, as well as their positions and the overall segment text, are specified in the log entry (see Figure 9). Furthermore, all log entries contain the modality of the interaction, e.g., speech or pen, thereby allowing the analysis of which modality was used for which editing operation. All log entries with timestamps are created within the client and sent to the server for storage in a JSON file.

We also worked on improvements and extensions to the logging functionality: Apart from bug fixes, we improved logs for copy and paste by adding the clipboard content, better distinguished between delete followed by an insert in comparison to replace operations, improved logs for reordering (distinction into reorder-single, reorder-group, and reorder-partial), and provided more understandable logs for undo/redo. Furthermore, we improved logging for multi-modal commands: We do not merely save whether the interaction was multi-modal, but store whether it was a combination of speech and pen, or speech and mouse, or speech and finger touch. Last, we plan to extend the logging functionality by adding gaze positions, fixations, and

{"type":"SPEECH_INPUT_ACTIVATION","interactionSource":"UI","interactionModality":"MOUSE","ts":1596114930776,"participant":1,"segmentID":5}
{"type":"DELETE_SINGLE","interactionModality":"SPEECH","interactionSource":"MICROPHONE","segmentTextOld":"\" Kunden, die früher ihre Vinyl verkauften, um CDs zu kaufen, verkaufen jetzt ihre CDs, um ihre Schallplatten zurückzukaufen\", sagt er.","segmentTextNew":"\" Kunden, die früher ihre verkauften, um CDs zu kaufen, verkaufen jetzt ihre CDs, um ihre Schallplatten zurückzukaufen\", sagt er.","position":"char:26","word":"Vinyl","ts":1596114957569,"participant":1,"segmentID":5}
{"type":"INSERT_SINGLE","interactionModality":"PEN","interactionSource":"IINK","segmentTextOld":"\" Kunden, die früher ihre verkauften, um CDs zu kaufen, verkaufen jetzt ihre CDs, um ihre Schallplatten zurückzukaufen\", sagt er.","segmentTextNew":"\" Kunden, die früher ihre Schallplatten verkauften, um CDs zu kaufen, verkaufen jetzt ihre CDs, um ihre Schallplatten zurückzukaufen\", sagt er.","position":"word6","word":"Schallplatten","ts":1596114997526,"participant":1,"segmentID":5}
{"type":"REPLACE_SINGLE","interactionModality":"KEYBOARD","interactionSource":"MAIN","segmentTextOld":"\" Kunden, die früher ihre Schallplatten verkauften, um CDs zu kaufen, verkaufen jetzt ihre CDs, um ihre Schallplatten zurückzukaufen\", sagt er.","segmentTextNew":"\" Kunden, die früher ihre Schallplatten verkauften, um CDs zu kaufen, verkaufen jetzt ihre CDs, um ihre Vinyl zurückzukaufen\", sagt er.","position":"word21","wordOld":"Schallplatten","wordNew":"Vinyl","ts":1596115019597,"participant":1,"segmentID":5}
{"type":"SEGMENT_CONFIRM","interactionModality":"MOUSE","interactionSource":"UI","segmentText":"\" Kunden, die früher ihre Schallplatten verkauften, um CDs zu kaufen, verkaufen jetzt ihre CDs, um ihre Vinyl zurückzukaufen\", sagt er.","duration":105170,"ts":1596115022794,"participant":1,"segmentID":5}
{"type":"SEGMENT_SELECT","interactionSource":"UI","interactionModality":"MOUSE","ts":1596115022799,"participant":1,"segmentID":6}

Figure 9: Logging of text manipulations in an easily interpretable granularity.

especially pupil diameter, which can be used for cognitive load analyses (Herbig et al., 2020a). Alongside these, we are planning on integrating further physiological sensors, e.g., the Empatica E4, to capture cognitive load more robustly in a multi-modal fashion by also considering factors like heart rate variability or skin conductance.

4 Conclusion and Future Work

Due to continuously improving MT systems, PE is becoming more and more relevant in modern-day translation. The interfaces used by translators still heavily focus on translation from scratch, and in particular on mouse and keyboard input modalities. Since PE requires less production of text but instead more error corrections, Herbig et al. (2020b) presented and evaluated the MMPE CAT environment that explores the use of speech commands, handwriting input, touch reordering, and multi-modal combinations for PE of MT. In this paper, we use the presented feedback from professional translators to improve and extend the existing prototype: We redesigned the layout, added visualization of whitespaces, fixed issues in hand-writing, allowed multi-word reordering using touch drag and drop and improved its visualization, extended the speech commands, provided better feedback for the user on what the speech commands changed, and improved the logging functionality. Furthermore, we showcased an early implementation of how eye tracking can be integrated, not only for logging but as an actual interaction modality that can be used in combination with speech recognition or the keyboard to quickly correct errors.

As next steps, we want to study how this changed prototype impacts the user experience. Furthermore, we want to finalize the eye-tracking implementation and run a study that specifically explores the combination of eye and speech/keyboard input for PE. Apart from that, longer-term studies exploring how the modality usage changes over time, whether users continuously switch modalities or stick to specific ones for specific tasks, are planned. Furthermore, as eye tracking is already integrated into the prototype for explicit interaction, we want to explore eye-based cognitive load detection and react to high levels of cognitive load by providing alternative MT proposals, as discussed in Herbig et al. (2019b). Finally, to transform MMPE into a fully fledged translation workbench, we want to add user and project management functionality, allow direct loading of common file types like .docx, and cover more language pairs.

References

Alabau, V., Bonk, R., Buck, C., Carl, M., Casacuberta, F., García-Martínez, M., González, J., Koehn, P., Leiva, L., Mesa-Lao, B., et al. (2013). CASMACAT: An open source workbench for advanced computer aided translation. *The Prague Bulletin of Mathematical Linguistics*, 100:101–112.

Alabau, V. and Casacuberta, F. (2012). Study of electronic pen commands for interactive-predictive machine translation. In *Proceedings of the International Workshop on Expertise in Translation and Post-Editing – Research and Application*, pages 17–18.

Aranberri, N., Labaka, G., Diaz de Ilarraza, A., and Sarasola, K. (2014). Comparison of post-editing productivity between professional translators and lay users. In *Proceeding of AMTA Third Workshop on Post-Editing Technology and Practice*, pages 20–33.

Brousseau, J., Drouin, C., Foster, G., Isabelle, P., Kuhn, R., Normandin, Y., and Plamondon, P. (1995). French speech recognition in an automatic dictation system for translators: The TransTalk project. In *Proceedings of Eurospeech Fourth European Conference on Speech Communication and Technology*, pages 193–196.

Carl, M., Jensen, M., and Kristian, K. (2010). Long distance revisions in drafting and post-editing. *CICLing Special Issue on Natural Language Processing and its Applications*, pages 193–204.

Coppers, S., van den Bergh, J., Luyten, K., Coninx, K., van der Lek-Ciudin, I., Vanallemeersch, T., and Vandeghinste, V. (2018). Intellingo: An intelligible translation environment. In *Proceedings of the SIGCHI Conference on Human Factors in Computing Systems*, pages 1–13. ACM.

Dymetman, M., Brousseau, J., Foster, G., Isabelle, P., Normandin, Y., and Plamondon, P. (1994). Towards an automatic dictation system for translators: The TransTalk project. In *Proceedings of the ICSLP International Conference on Spoken Language Processing*.

Federico, M., Bertoldi, N., Cettolo, M., Negri, M., Turchi, M., Trombetti, M., Cattelan, A., Farina, A., Lupinetti, D., Martines, A., et al. (2014). The MateCat tool. In *Proceedings of the 25th International Conference on Computational Linguistics: System Demonstrations*, pages 129–132.

Gaspari, F., Toral, A., Naskar, S. K., Groves, D., and Way, A. (2014). Perception vs reality: Measuring machine translation post-editing productivity. In *Third Workshop on Post-Editing Technology and Practice*, page 60.

Green, S., Chuang, J., Heer, J., and Manning, C. D. (2014a). Predictive translation memory: A mixed-initiative system for human language translation. In *Proceedings of the 27th Annual ACM Symposium on User Interface Software and Technology*, pages 177–187. ACM.

Green, S., Heer, J., and Manning, C. D. (2013). The efficacy of human post-editing for language translation. In *Proceedings of the SIGCHI Conference on Human Factors in Computing Systems*, pages 439–448. ACM.

Green, S., Wang, S. I., Chuang, J., Heer, J., Schuster, S., and Manning, C. D. (2014b). Human effort and machine learnability in computer aided translation. In *Proceedings of the EMNLP Conference on Empirical Methods in Natural Language Processing*, pages 1225–1236.

Herbig, N., Düwel, T., Helali, M., Eckhart, L., Schuck, P., Choudhury, S., and Krüger, A. (2020a). Investigating multi-modal measures for cognitive load detection in e-learning. In *Proceedings of the 28th ACM Conference on User Modeling, Adaptation and Personalization*, pages 88–97.

Herbig, N., Düwel, T., Pal, S., Meladaki, K., Monshizadeh, M., Krüger, A., and van Genabith, J. (2020b). MMPE: A multi-modal interface for post-editing machine translation. In *Proceedings of the 58th Annual Meeting of the Association for Computational Linguistics*, pages 1691–1702. Association for Computational Linguistics.

Herbig, N., Pal, S., Düwel, T., Meladaki, K., Monshizadeh, M., Hnatovskiy, V., Krüger, A., and van Genabith, J. (2020c). MMPE: A multi-modal interface using handwriting, touch reordering, and speech commands for post-editing machine translation. In *Proceedings of the 58th Annual Meeting of the Association for Computational Linguistics: System Demonstrations*, pages 327–334. Association for Computational Linguistics.

Herbig, N., Pal, S., van Genabith, J., and Krüger, A. (2019a). Multi-modal approaches for post-editing machine translation. In *Proceedings of the SIGCHI Conference on Human Factors in Computing Systems*, page 231. ACM.

Herbig, N., Pal, S., Vela, M., Krüger, A., and Genabith, J. (2019b). Multi-modal indicators for estimating perceived cognitive load in post-editing of machine translation. *Machine Translation*, 33(1-2):91–115.

Kern, D., Marshall, P., and Schmidt, A. (2010). Gazemarks: Gaze-based visual placeholders to ease attention switching. In *Proceedings of the SIGCHI Conference on Human Factors in Computing Systems*, pages 2093–2102. ACM.

Koponen, M. (2012). Comparing human perceptions of post-editing effort with post-editing operations. In *Proceedings of the Seventh Workshop on Statistical Machine Translation*, pages 181–190. Association for Computational Linguistics.

Lagoudaki, E. (2009). Translation editing environments. In *MT Summit XII: Workshop on Beyond Translation Memories*.

Läubli, S., Fishel, M., Massey, G., Ehrensberger-Dow, M., and Volk, M. (2013). Assessing post-editing efficiency in a realistic translation environment. In *Proceedings of MT Summit XIV Workshop on Post-Editing Technology and Practice*, pages 83–91.

Martinez, M. G., Singla, K., Tammewar, A., Mesa-Lao, B., Thakur, A., Anusuya, M., Srinivas, B., and Carl, M. (2014). SEECAT: ASR & eye-tracking enabled computer assisted translation. In *The 17th Annual Conference of the European Association for Machine Translation*, pages 81–88. European Association for Machine Translation.

Mesa-Lao, B. (2014). Speech-enabled computer-aided translation: A satisfaction survey with post-editor trainees. In *Proceedings of the EACL 2014 Workshop on Humans and Computer-Assisted Translation*, pages 99–103.

Moorkens, J. (2018). What to expect from neural machine translation: A practical in-class translation evaluation exercise. *The Interpreter and Translator Trainer*, 12(4):375–387.

Moorkens, J. and O'Brien, S. (2015). Post-editing evaluations: Trade-offs between novice and professional participants. In *Proceedings of the 18th Annual Conference of the European Association for Machine Translation*, pages 75–81.

Moorkens, J. and O'Brien, S. (2017). Assessing user interface needs of post-editors of machine translation. In *Human Issues in Translation Technology*, pages 127–148. Routledge.

O'Brien, S., Moorkens, J., and Vreeke, J. (2014). Kanjingo – a mobile app for post-editing. In *Proceedings of the 17th Annual Conference of the European Association for Machine Translation*.

Schwartz, L., Lacruz, I., and Bystrova, T. (2015). Effects of word alignment visualization on post-editing quality & speed. *Proceedings of MT Summit XV*, 1:186–199.

Sindhwani, S., Lutteroth, C., and Weber, G. (2019). ReType: Quick text editing with keyboard and gaze. In *Proceedings of the 2019 CHI Conference on Human Factors in Computing Systems*, pages 1–13.

Teixeira, C. S., Moorkens, J., Turner, D., Vreeke, J., and Way, A. (2019). Creating a multimodal translation tool and testing machine translation integration using touch and voice. *Informatics*, 6.

Theologitis, D. (1998). Language tools at the EC translation service: The theory and the practice. In *Proceedings of the 20th Conference Translating and the Computer*, pages 12–13.

Toral, A., Wieling, M., and Way, A. (2018). Post-editing effort of a novel with statistical and neural machine translation. *Frontiers in Digital Humanities*, 5:9.

Torres-Hostench, O., Moorkens, J., O'Brien, S., Vreeke, J., et al. (2017). Testing interaction with a mobile MT post-editing app. *Translation & Interpreting*, 9(2):138.

van den Bergh, J., Geurts, E., Degraen, D., Haesen, M., van der Lek-Ciudin, I., Coninx, K., et al. (2015). Recommendations for translation environments to improve translators' workflows. In *Proceedings of the 37th Conference Translating and the Computer*, pages 106–119. Tradulex.

Vandeghinste, V., Vanallemeersch, T., Augustinus, L., Bulté, B., Van Eynde, F., Pelemans, J., Verwimp, L., Wambacq, P., Heyman, G., Moens, M.-F., et al. (2019). Improving the translation environment for professional translators. *Informatics*, 6(2):24.

Vandeghinste, V., Vanallemeersch, T., Augustinus, L., Pelemans, J., Heyman, G., van der Lek-Ciudin, I., Tezcan, A., Degraen, D., van den Bergh, J., Macken, L., et al. (2016). Scate – Smart Computer-Aided Translation Environment. *Baltic Journal of Modern Computing*, 4(2):382–382.

Vela, M., Pal, S., Zampieri, M., Naskar, S. K., and van Genabith, J. (2019). Improving CAT tools in the translation workflow: New approaches and evaluation. In *Proceedings of Machine Translation Summit XVII Volume 2: Translator, Project and User Tracks*, pages 8–15.

Wallis, J. (2006). *Interactive Translation vs Pre-translation in the Context of Translation Memory Systems: Investigating the Effects of Translation Method on Productivity, Quality and Translator Satisfaction.* PhD thesis, University of Ottawa.

Yamada, M. (2015). Can college students be post-editors? An investigation into employing language learners in machine translation plus post-editing settings. *Machine Translation*, 29(1):49–67.

Zampieri, M. and Vela, M. (2014). Quantifying the influence of MT output in the translators' performance: A case study in technical translation. In *Proceedings of the EACL 2014 Workshop on Humans and Computer-Assisted Translation*, pages 93–98.

Zapata, J. (2016). Translating on the go? Investigating the potential of multimodal mobile devices for interactive translation dictation. *Tradumàtica: Traducció i Tecnologies de la Informació i la Comunicació*, 1(14):66–74.

Zapata, J., Castilho, S., and Moorkens, J. (2017). Translation dictation vs. post-editing with cloud-based voice recognition: A pilot experiment. *Proceedings of MT Summit XVI*, 2.

Zaretskaya, A. and Seghiri, M. (2018). *User Perspective on Translation Tools: Findings of a User Survey.* PhD thesis, University of Malaga.

Zaretskaya, A., Vela, M., Pastor, G. C., and Seghiri, M. (2016). Comparing post-editing difficulty of different machine translation errors in Spanish and German translations from English. *International Journal of Language and Linguistics*, 3(3):91–100.

Translation vs Post-editing of NMT Output: Measuring effort in the English-Greek language pair

Maria Stasimioti   stasimioti@ionio.gr

Department of Foreign Languages, Translation and Interpreting, Ionian University, Corfu, 49100, Greece

Vilelmini Sosoni   sosoni@ionio.gr

Department of Foreign Languages, Translation and Interpreting, Ionian University, Corfu, 49100, Greece

Abstract

Machine Translation (MT) has been increasingly used in industrial translation production scenarios thanks to the development of Neural Machine Translation (NMT) models and the improvement of MT output, especially at the level of fluency. In particular, in an effort to speed up the translation process and reduce costs, MT output is used as raw translation to be subsequently post-edited by translators. However, post-editing (PE) has been found to differ from both human translation and revision of human translation in terms of the cognitive processes and the practical goals and processes employed. In addition, translators remain sceptical towards PE and question its real benefits. The paper seeks to investigate the effort required for full PE and compare it with the effort required for manual translation, focusing on the English-Greek language pair and NMT output. In particular, eye-tracking and keystroke logging data are used to measure the effort expended by translators while translating from scratch and the effort required while post-editing the NMT output. The findings indicate that the effort is lower when post-editing than when translating from scratch, while they also suggest that experience in PE plays a role.

1. Introduction

In the past fifteen years, the translation industry has seen a growth in the amount of content to be translated and has received pressure to increase productivity and speed at reduced costs. To respond to these challenges, it has turned to Machine Translation (MT). The most common and widely expanding scenario —especially for certain language pairs and domains— involves the use of MT output to be then post-edited by professional translators (Koponen, 2016). This practice —generally termed post-editing of machine translation (PEMT) or simply post-editing (PE)— is increasingly gaining ground (Green et al., 2013; O'Brien et al., 2014; O'Brien and Simard, 2014; Lommel and DePalma 2016; Vieira et al. 2019) not least because of the development of Neural Machine Translation (NMT) models and the subsequent improvement of MT output, especially at the level of fluency (Castilho et al., 2017). In fact, studies have shown that post-editing high-quality MT output can, indeed, increase the productivity of professional translators compared to manual translation, i.e. human translation or translation "from scratch" (cf. O'Brien 2007; Groves and Schmidtke 2009; Tatsumi 2009; Guerberof, 2009; Plitt and Masselot, 2010). However, PE has been found to differ from both human translation and revision of human translation in terms of the cognitive processes and the practical goals and processes employed (Krings, 2001; O'Brien, 2002), while translators approach it with caution and skepticism and question its real benefits (Gaspari et al., 2014; Koponen, 2012; Moorkens, 2018; Vieira and Alonso, 2018). Their skepticism is directly related to the nature of PE which involves "working by correction rather than creation" (Wagner, 1985: 2), to the perception that PEMT is slower than translating from scratch and to the fear that MT is a threat to their profession (Moorkens, 2018) and "might have a de-professionalising effect on translation" (Vieira and Alonso, 2018: 16). It is, thus, particularly interesting to investigate the productivity gains when post-editing NMT output and to measure the cognitive effort expended by post-editors during the PE task and determine whether the translators' skepticism is justified or whether translating by PE is indeed the way forward (Garcia, 2011).

Under the light of the above, the aim of the paper is to investigate the effort required for the full PE of NMT output and compare it with the effort required for manual translation, focusing on the English-Greek language pair. To that end, twelve experienced professional translators are asked to post-edit NMT output of two semi-specialised texts and also manually translate two different comparable texts. Eye-tracking and keystroke logging data are used in order to measure the effort expended by translators while translating from scratch and the effort required while carrying out full PE of the NMT output.

2. Related work

Lately, many studies have showcased the benefits of post-editing MT output, as opposed to translating source texts (STs) from scratch, mainly in the context of non-literary translation (cf. O'Brien 2007; Groves and Schmidtke 2009; Tatsumi 2009; Green et al., 2013; Plitt and Masselot, 2010), but also in the context of literary translation (cf. Genzel et al., 2010; Greene et al., 2010; Jones and Irvine 2013; Besacier, 2014; Toral and Way, 2015; Moorkens et al., 2018). More specifically, several studies have been carried out with a view to estimating the productivity gains when post-editing MT output and measuring the cognitive effort expended by post-editors. In particular, Plitt and Masselot (2010) carried out a productivity test involving PE of MT output compared to traditional human translation in an industrial environment and found that MT helped translators substantially improve their productivity given that MT followed by PE improved throughput on average by 74%, thus reducing translation time by 43%. In a similar study, Zhechev (2014) found that MT followed by PE resulted in substantial productivity gains as compared to translation from scratch.

However, productivity alone does not provide information on "how post-editing occurs as ı process, how it is distinguished from conventional translation, what demands it makes on post-editors, and what kind of acceptance it receives from them" (Krings 2001: 61). Therefore, Krings (2001) argues that the feasibility of post-editing compared to human translating should not be determined by processing time alone. O'Brien (2011: 198) also claims that post-editing productivity means "not only the ratio of quantity and quality to time but also the cognitive effort expended; and the higher the effort, the lower the productivity". More specifically, Krings (2001) identifies three categories of PE effort: the temporal effort, which refers to the time taken to post-edit a sentence to a particular level of quality, the technical effort, which refers to keystroke and mouse activities such as deletions, insertions, and text re-ordering and the cognitive effort, which refers to the "type and extent of those cognitive processes that must be activated in order to remedy a given deficiency in a machine translation" (Krings, 2001: 179). Therefore, research into the cognitive aspect of PE is necessary for a better understanding of PE effort and its relation to that of conventional translation. Under that light, a series of studies have tried to investigate the cognitive effort in relation to PE and manual translation (e.g. Carl et al., 2011;

Balling and Carl, 2014; Mesa-Lao, 2014; Elming, Balling and Carl, 2014; Carl, Gutermuth and Hansen-Schira, 2015, Jia et al., 2019).

The above studies compare manual translation with PE of Statistical Machine Translation (SMT) and NMT outputs. The present study's novelty is the focus on the English-Greek language pair for which there are no related studies to date.

3. Experimental setup

As already pointed out, eye-tracking and keystroke logging data were used to measure the temporal, technical and cognitive effort expended by translators while translating from scratch and while carrying out full PE of the NMT output. The translation and PE experiments were carried out in March 2018 at the HUBIC Lab[1] (Raptis and Giagkou, 2016) of the Athena Research Center[2] in Athens. A detailed consent form was signed by all participants prior to the execution of the experiments, while all stored data were fully anonymized in accordance with Greek Law 2472/97 (as amended by Laws 3783/2009, 3917/2011 and 4070/2012).

Twelve Greek professional translators participated in the experiments, in which their eye movements and typing activity were registered with the help of an eye-tracker and specialised software. Their selection followed a call for participation which was sent to the members of the two biggest Greek associations of professional translators, i.e. the Panhellenic Association of Translators[3] (PEM) and Panhellenic Association of Professional Translation Graduates of the Ionian University[4] (PEEMPIP) and was shared on social media. Potential participants expressed their interest for participating in the study by filling in a Google form; they subsequently received an e-mail with details on the aim of the research and guidelines for the translation and PE task along with some educational material (see section 3.2). In addition, they were asked to fill in two questionnaires: a pre-task questionnaire and a post-task questionnaire. The pre-task questionnaire, consisting of 34 questions (22 closed-ended questions and 12 open-ended questions), aimed at defining the profile of the participants and their perception of MT and had to be filled in before the experiment, while the post-task questionnaire, consisting of 15 questions (13 closed-ended questions and 2 open-ended questions), aimed at receiving feedback on translation and PE tasks and had to be filled in after the experiment.

3.1. The participants

As it emerges from Table 1, all the participants were female. Half of them were aged 30 to 40 years old, 33% were aged 40-50 years old and 17% were aged 20-30 years old. The majority of the participants had either an undergraduate degree (42%) or a postgraduate degree (50%), mainly in the translation field (67%). It should also be noted that all participants had normal or corrected to normal vision, two wore contact lenses, and one wore glasses, yet the calibration with the eye-tracker was successful for all twelve.

Gender	Female	100%
	Male	0%
Age group distribution	20-30	17%
	30-40	50%

---

[1] http://www.hubic-lab.eu/

[2] https://www.athenarc.gr/en

[3] http://www.pem.gr/el/

[4] http://peempip.gr/el/

	40-50	33%
Education level	Undergraduate degree holders	42%
	Postgraduate degree holders	50%
	PhD holders	8%
Degree type	Translation	67%
	Language/Linguistics	25%
	Other	8%

Table 1. Participants' age distribution, education level and degree type

The majority (83%) had at least 5 years of experience in translation (Table 2), while their work involved translation tasks (100%), revision tasks (92%), PE tasks (67%), terminology work (50%) project management (50%), subtitling (33%) as well as other tasks (17%) (Table 3).

	1-5 years	17%
Years of experience in translation	5-10 years	17%
	10-20 years	58%
	> 20 years	8%

Table 2. Participants' years of experience in translation

	Translating	100%
	Revising	92%
	Post-editing	67%
Tasks involved in participants' work	Project Management	50%
	Terminology work	50%
	Subtitling	33%
	Other	17%

Table 3. Tasks involved in participants' work

As far as their experience in PE is concerned, 84% of participants had experience in PE, either 1 year (25%), 2 years (17%), 3 years (17%), 5 years (17%) or over 5 years (8%) of experience in PE (Table 4).

	0 years	16%
	1 year	25%
	2 years	17%
Years of experience in PE	3 years	17%
	4 years	0%
	5 years	17%
	> 5 years	8%

Table 4. Participants' years of experience in PE

However, when they were asked about their workload ratio involving the PE of MT output, more than half replied that PE involved only 1% to 25% of the daily workload. For one of them PE involved 26% to 50% of the daily workload, for another one PE involved 51% to 75% of the daily workload, while for 3 of them PE involved 0% of the daily workload (Table 5).

	0%	25%
	1 - 25%	59%
Participants' workload ratio involving post-editing MT output	26 - 50%	8%
	51 - 75%	8%
	76 - 100%	0%

Table 5. Participants' workload ratio involving post-editing MT output

Although a high percentage of the participants, namely 84%, declared that they had previous experience in PE, only 33% of them had received training in PE, while 83% would be interested in receiving training in PE, saying that they consider it to be either moderately important (58%) or very important (42%) (Table 6). In addition, 75% of the participants stated that they prefer not to use MT in their CAT tools (Table 7).

	Extremely important	0%
	Very important	42%
Participants' view on PE training	Moderately important	58%
	Not important	0%
	Not at all important	0%

Table 6. Participants' view on PE training

Use of MT in participant's work	Yes	25%
	No	75%

Table 7. Use of MT in participants' work

Their answers to these two questions are closely related to their answers about their perception towards PE and MT, since a positive attitude to MT has been found to be a factor in PE performance (de Almeida, 2013; Mitchell, 2015). In particular, their answers regarding their perception towards PE were mixed. Some of them believed that PE is a useful, time-saving and necessary task, going hand in hand with MT and they were willing to add it to their services. However, others were negatively disposed stating that they preferred translation from scratch, that PE made their job harder and that PE rates were not fair. It should be noted that those negatively disposed were mainly translators with many years of experience or translators working predominantly with marketing texts or transcreation. This is in line with the findings of Moorkens and O'Brien (2015), who also observed that attitudes appear to be more negative in the case of experienced translators. As regards their perception towards MT and although the majority pointed out that they prefer not to use MT in their CAT tools, many appeared to recognise the latest developments in the field stating that "[MT] has done huge steps forward in the past years. Definitely here to stay. And to be used more with AI applications"; "MT can offer significant improvements in speed and accuracy when the machine is trained with good quality data", while as far as Google Translate is concerned "[It is] very useful and getting better by the day. I am happy to use it for languages I do not know, I may not always feel 100% positive about it as a professional linguist, but I accept it for what it is". It should be noted that the participants who were negatively disposed to PE were also negatively disposed to MT.

Regarding the translation and PE task difficulty, as this was identified by them in the post-task questionnaire, the participants found both tasks to be neither very easy nor very difficult. The User Interface (Translog II environment), the STs' difficulty and the quality of the MT raw output were among the factors that posed problems to the participants during the translation task and the PE task respectively. There were, also, other reasons that caused difficulties in both tasks such as the inability of the participants to consult dictionaries and external resources.

3.2. Description of the experiment

A Tobii TX-300 eye-tracker[5] and Translog-II software (Carl, 2012) were used to register the participants' eye movements, keystrokes and time needed during the translation and PE tasks they were asked to carry out. The texts (see below) were displayed in 17-point Tahoma font and double spacing on a Tobii TX Display (23'') at 1920 x 1080 pixels and the average viewing distance aimed at was 50-60 cm from the screen.

According to O'Brien (2009) the quality of the eye-tracking data may be affected by several factors, such as participants' optical aids, eye make-up, lighting conditions, noise, unfamiliarity, user's distance from the monitor etc. In an effort to minimize the implications of some of these factors, a controlled environment for the experiment was set up. In particular, a quiet room was selected, blackout blinds were used to reduce the amount of natural light, the same artificial light was used during all experiments, and a fixed chair was used, so that the participants could not easily move about and increase or decrease the distance to the monitor (Hvelplund, 2011).

The experiment consisted of one session for each participant. Before the sessions, the participants were informed by email about the nature of the experiments, the task requirements and the general as well as task-specific guidelines they had to follow. More specifically, the general guidelines they received included the following:

- Your hair should not block your eyes.
- Do not wear mascara.
- Avoid touching your eyes (e.g. rubbing your eyes, removing/wearing eyeglasses, etc.).
- During the translation and PE tasks, look exclusively at the computer screen.
- Try to keep your head as steady as possible.
- External resources (dictionaries, Internet, etc.) cannot be used.

The translation task was a traditional manual translation assignment. Participants were asked to provide their translation in a split-screen window. The ST was displayed at the top half of the screen and the translation at the bottom half, as suggested by previous studies (Hvelplund, 2011; Carl et al., 2011; Mesa-Lao, 2014; Carl et al., 2015). Since all the participants in this study were professional translators, the only guideline provided to them was to produce a text with the same *skopos* (Vermeer, 1989) as that of the original text and of publishable quality.

The PE task was a traditional PE assignment. Participants were asked to fully post-edit the raw output generated by the NMT-core engine. Like in the translation task, the ST was displayed at the top half of the screen and the translation at the bottom half, as suggested by previous studies (Hvelplund, 2011; Carl et al., 2011; Mesa-Lao, 2014; Carl et al., 2015). Translators worked directly on the translation. To facilitate eye-tracking measurements, texts were fully displayed to avoid any need for participants to scroll in either the source (ST) or the target text (TT) window. As opposed to the translation task, they were given detailed guidelines as well as training material in PE. In particular, since previous training and experience in PE was not a prerequisite for participating in the study, the participants received brief training in PE before executing the task. The training included a video, a presentation, as well as some educational material in PE which were sent to them five days before the execution of the tasks. The

---

[5] The TX-300 eye tracker is an integrated eye tracker that is supplied with a removable 23'' TFT monitor. Its large head movement box allows the subject to move during tracking while maintaining accuracy and precision at a sampling rate of 300 Hz. (https://www.tobiipro.com/product-listing/tobii-pro-tx300/).

guidelines for the full PE of the NMT output were based on the comparative overview of full PE guidelines provided by Hu and Cadwell (2016) as these were proposed by TAUS (2016), O'Brien (2010), Flanagan and Christensen (2014), Mesa-Lao (2013) and Densmer (2014), i.e retain as much raw MT translation/output as possible, the message transferred should be accurate, fix any omissions and/or additions (at the level of sentence, phrase or word), correct mistranslations, correct morphological errors, correct misspellings and typos, fix incorrect punctuation if it interferes with the message, correct wrong terminology, fix inconsistent use of terms, do not introduce stylistic changes.

In an effort to ensure that they had actually studied the material and that there were no questions or doubts, the participants were interviewed prior to the execution of the tasks and were specifically asked about the training material and also about the guidelines they had received.

A warm-up task was completed for human translation before the translation task and a warm-up task for PE before the actual PE task. The participants were informed that data from all texts would be subjected to analysis, although the warm-up texts were used only in order to familiarize the participants with the environment, the tools and the different types of tasks. After the warm-up, the actual experimental tasks followed, which involved the translation of two texts, i.e Text 1 and Text 2 (see below), and the PE of two different texts, i.e Text 3 and Text 4 see below), following the afore-mentioned guidelines. Participants were also asked to carry out both tasks at the speed at which they would normally work in their everyday work as professional translators; therefore, no time constraint was imposed. However, access to either online or offline translation aids was not allowed as it could have led to a reduction in the amount of recorded eye-tracking data.

The English STs used in this study were short educational texts selected from OER Commons[6], which is a public digital library of open educational resources. Six[7] 120 to 140-word long excerpts were selected from various courses on Business Administration and Social Change and the titles of the courses were retained as context information for the participants. The texts were chosen with the following criteria in mind: they had to be semi-specialised and easy for participants to translate or post-edit without access to external resources and they also had to be of comparable complexity. The texts chosen had comparable Lexile®[8] scores per task (between 1000L and 1100L for the translation task and 1300L and 1400L for the PE task), i.e they were suitable for 11th/12th graders (Table 8).

	Text 1 – T1	Text 2 – T2	Text 3 – T3	Text 4 – T4
Lexile® Measure	1000L - 1100L	1000L - 1100L	1300L - 1400L	1300L - 1400L
Number of sentences	8	8	6	7
Mean sentence length	15.38	17.43	28.60	22.67
Word count	123	122	143	136
Characters without spaces	777	713	785	896

Table 8. Lexile® scores for the source texts used in the study

---

[6] https://www.oercommons.org/
[7] Two texts were used exclusively for the warm-up session and are not included in the ensuing analysis and discussion.
[8] https://la-tools.lexile.com/free-analyze/

The NMT-core engine used to produce the Greek raw MT output for the PE task was Google Translate (output obtained March 24, 2018). The NMT output was evaluated using the BLEU and WER metrics. The BLEU score was calculated using the Tilde Custom Machine Translation toolkit[9]. As it emerges from Table 9, both texts had a very good score as regards BLEU and WER score and PE could be used to achieve publishable translation quality.

Text	Translation engine	BLEU	WER
Economics – Text 3	Google Translate NMT	51.33	37.7
The Endocrine System – Text 4	Google Translate NMT	60.62	34.5

Table 9. Automatic evaluation scores per text

4. Measuring translation and PE cognitive effort

As already pointed out, eye-tracking and keystroke logging data were used to calculate the participants' effort, i.e. the temporal effort, the technical effort and the cognitive effort which was expended during the translation and PE tasks.

4.1. Temporal Effort

According to Carl et al. (2011: 137) "One of the most obvious reasons for engaging in post-editing is the desire to save time". In his study the average time spent on manually translating a text was 7.52 minutes, while the average time spent on post-editing a text was 7.35 minutes. Although that difference was not significant ($p = 0.7118$), Carl et al. considered it "an indication that post-editing may lead to some time saving" (Carl et al., 2011: 137). In our study, we observed a statistically significant difference $t(23) = 3.04$, $p < 0.01$, when comparing the average task time[10] required for the translation task ($M = 9.86$, $SD = 4.53$) and the PE task *($M = 7.91$, $SD = 2.48$)* (Table 10), resulting, thus, in an average time saving[11] of 19.8%. It is worth noting that the study' s findings corroborate the findings of previous studies which, however, involve different language pairs, MT systems, participants and experimental set-ups. In particular, the 19.8% average time saving percentage is similar to the 25% average time saving reported by Elming et al. (2014). According to Mesa-Lao (2014), who also found that translators in his study were always faster in the PE task, the longer task time in the translation task may be explained by the requirement of the translators to first read the ST (initial orientation phase) before starting to type the translation (drafting phase). When translating from scratch there are three phases: initial orientation (reading), translation drafting and final revision (Mesa-Lao, 2014; Carl et al., 2011). When post-editing, though, most post-editors tend to skip the initial orientation phase, in an effort to save time and they also tend to skip overall the final revision phase after making their changes, since PE is a kind of revision of the machine generated text (Mesa-Lao, 2014). So, according to Mesa-Lao (2014), this lack of a clear orientation phase and revision phase, along with the fact that (in principle) much less typing should be involved in PE when compared to translation, may explain the differences in task times.

Carl et al. (2015) and Jia et al. (2019) measured the average per-word translation and PE time in milliseconds (ms) and also found PE to be faster than translation from scratch. Although the participants in both studies had no previous experience in PE, they needed less time for PE,

---

[9] https://www.letsmt.eu/Bleu.aspx

[10] It should be noted that the start time of the task was calculated from the moment we opened the project (i.e. when we pressed the "start logging" button) and the task was considered finished when we pressed the "stop logging" button.

[11] Time saved percentage = 100 - average PE time/average translation time*100 (Elming et al., 2014)

leading Carl et al. (2015: 168) to make the assumption that "trained post-editors would even be more efficient in terms of editing times". A similar assumption, i.e. "more post-editing experience will yield a margin of time saving", was made in another previous study (Carl et al., 2011: 138), where also no participant had previous experience in PE. In our case, the majority (84%) of the participants had previous experience in PE (see section 3.1). When measuring the average task time expended by the participants with previous experience in PE and comparing it to the average task time expended by those without previous experience in PE (Table 11), we noticed that the experience in PE had affected the time the participants needed to post-edit the two texts (Text 3 and Text 4). In particular, the average task time expended by the participants with previous experience in PE was 7.07 minutes, while the average task time expended by those without previous experience was 10.42 minutes (Table 11). Although that difference is not significant ($p = 0.11$) –due to the low number of the participants and the number of texts involved in this study– it still indicates that PE experience may lead to lower temporal effort.

Task	Mean	SD
Translation task	9.86	4.53
PE task	7.91	2.48

Table 10. Temporal effort per task: Mean and standard deviation values of the task duration

Task	Participants	Mean	SD
PE	Professionals with experience in PE	7.07	1.34
	Professionals without experience in PE	10.42	4.09

Table 11. Professionals with experience in PE vs professionals without experience in PE: Mean and standard deviation values of the PE task duration

4.2. Technical Effort

Although it goes without saying that translation requires more typing than PE, given that one starts from scratch, it is interesting to compare the technical effort, i.e. the number of keystrokes (insertions and deletions), involved in both activities as the findings are useful in terms of ergonomics related to the translators' overall well-being and acceptance of MT and PE. The study reveals a statistically significant difference $t\,(23) = 16.08$, $p < 0.01$ between the average keyboard activity in the translation task ($M = 1195$, $SD = 126$) and the PE task ($M = 458$, $SD = 226$) (Table 12). In line with Carl et al. (2011), we noticed that the number of insertions was higher in the translation task, while the number of deletions was higher in the PE task. This can be easily explained by the fact that in the translation task the participants performed the translation from scratch, whereas in the PE task they only corrected the errors from the machine generated output. Interestingly, deletions were quite high in the translation task. This may be (partly) due to the participants' inability to consult external resources, a fact that led them to delete and rewrite words of their own translations in an effort to produce a better translation, as well as due to typos they had to correct while translating.

The experience in PE seems also to have affected the technical effort (Table 13). In particular, in the PE task the average keyboard activity of the participants with previous experience in PE was 438 keystrokes and for those without experience 521 keystrokes. Although the difference between the average keyboard activity is not significant ($p = 0.52$), it indicates that experienced post-editors may perform less keystrokes than those without experience in PE.

Task	Total number of keystrokes		Insertions		Deletions	
	Mean	SD	Mean	SD	Mean	SD
Translation	1195	126	1039	70	156	62
PE	458	226	239	116	220	111

Table 12. Technical effort per task: Mean and standard deviation values for the total number of keystrokes, insertions and deletions

Task	Participants	Total number of keystrokes		Insertions		Deletions	
		Mean	SD	Mean	SD	Mean	SD
PE	Professionals with experience in PE	438	211	228	110	209	103
	Professionals without experience in PE	521	279	270	140	252	138

Table 13. Professionals with experience in PE vs professionals without experience in PE: Mean and standard deviation values for the total number of keystrokes, insertions and deletions in the PE task

4.3. Cognitive effort

Eye-tracking measures, such as fixation count, fixation duration, gaze time, pupil dilation and saccades, have been lately used for measuring cognitive effort in translation studies (Moorkens, 2018). In particular, an increased number of fixations (Doherty et al., 2010), longer average fixation durations (Carl et al., 2011) and gaze time, i.e. the sum of all fixation durations, (Sharmin et al., 2008) have been used as indicators of particular items requiring more cognitive effort. In the present study and similarly to Mesa Lao (2014), we noticed that the translation task triggered more ($M = 1284$, $SD = 791$) and longer ($M = 420$, $SD = 70.38$) fixations than the PE task ($M = 1135$, $SD = 429$ and $M = 355$, $SD = 37.75$ respectively) (Table 14). The differences in average fixation count ($p = 0.17$) and fixation duration ($t(23) = 5.46$, $p < 0.01$) indicate that the cognitive load is higher in the translation task than in the PE task. Contrary to Carl et al. (2011), who found the average gaze time to be almost the same in the manual translation task and in the PE task, we found in our study a statistically significant difference $t(23) = 3.27$, $p < 0.01$ between the average gaze time in the translation task ($M = 8.44$, $SD = 3.94$) and in the PE task ($M = 6.62$, $SD = 2.18$) (Table 14). Therefore, it is obvious from our findings that PE is less cognitively demanding than translation from scratch. Similarly to our findings in the case of temporal effort (section 4.1) and technical effort (section 4.2), previous experience seems to have also affected the cognitive effort. In particular, a difference in fixation count ($p = 0.18$) and gaze time ($p = 0.19$) was found between the participants with previous experience in PE ($M = 1020$ and $M = 6.05$ respectively) and those without previous experience in PE ($M = 1480$ and $M = 8.31$ respectively), indicating that the cognitive load might be lower for experienced post-editors (Table 15).

	Fixation count		Fixation duration (msec)		Total gaze time (mins)	
Task	Mean	SD	Mean	SD	Mean	SD
Translation	1284	791	420	70.38	8.44	3.94
PE	1135	429	355	37.75	6.62	2.18

Table14. Cognitive effort per task: Mean and standard deviation values of the fixation count, the fixation duration and the gaze time

Task	Participants	Fixation count		Fixation duration (msec)		Total gaze time (mins)	
		Mean	SD	Mean	SD	Mean	SD
PE	Professionals with experience in PE	1020	202	345.68	43.99	6.05	1.16
	Professionals without experience in PE	1480	719	358.30	36.39	8.31	3.56

Table 13. Professionals with experience in PE vs professionals without experience in PE: Mean and standard deviation values of the fixation count, the fixation duration and the gaze time in the PE task

Looking at the distribution of visual attention between the ST and TT areas, we noticed that in the translation task the fixation count ($M = 751$, $SD = 467$) and the gaze time ($M = 4.41$, $SD = 2.28$) were higher in the ST areas than in the TT areas ($M = 533$, $SD = 323$ and $M = 4.03$, $SD = 1.64$ respectively) (Table 16) presumably due to more careful reading and understanding of the ST, as well as due to the translators' need not only to feed their brain with input for meaning construction but also to monitor while typing that the TT conveys the meaning of the ST (Carl et al., 2011 and Mesa-Lao, 2014). In line with the findings of previous studies (Mesa-Lao, 2014 and Carl et al., 2011), in the PE task, the fixations ($M = 386$, $SD = 144$) and the gaze time ($M = 1.95$, $SD = 0.72$) on the ST areas decrease considerably, while much of the activity involved in the task takes place in the TT area ($M = 748$, $SD = 303$ and $M = 4.67$, $SD = 1.43$ respectively) (Table 16). According to Elming et al. (2014: 161), this is not surprising since "translation suggestion is already presented for post-editing, so less inspiration from looking at the source is needed". In line with the findings of a previous study (Carl et al., 2011), the number of fixations in the translation task was, in most cases, distributed more evenly on the ST and the TT areas than in the PE task, where the majority of the participants (9 out of 12) had almost twice as many fixations on the TT areas than on the ST areas.

Task	Fixation count				Total gaze time (mins)			
	ST area		TT area		ST area		TT area	
	Mean	SD	Mean	SD	Mean	SD	Mean	SD
Translation	751	467	533	323	4.41	2.28	4.03	1.64
PE	386	144	748	303	1.95	0.72	4.67	1.43

Table 146. Cognitive effort per task: Mean and standard deviation values of the fixation count and the gaze time per text area

5. Conclusions and Future Work

Although the sample is small, taking into account the length of the texts and the number of participants, our initial study indicates clearly that the effort needed by professional translators when post-editing NMT output is less than the effort required when translating comparable texts from scratch. In particular, the study showed that professional translators needed less time (temporal effort) for post-editing NMT output compared to the time required for translating from scratch, leading, thus, to a time saving of almost 20%. Keyboard activity (technical effort) was almost triple in the translation task, where insertions were more and deletions were less than in the PE task. Furthermore, the analysis reveals a higher cognitive effort in the translation task, with more and longer fixations and higher average gaze time. When translating from scratch, a more careful reading and a better understanding of the ST is evident from the higher fixation count and total gaze time on the ST area. In the PE task, on the other hand, much of the activity took place in the TT area.

Another interesting finding that emerges from the study is that professional translators with experience in PE expend less temporal, technical and cognitive effort during PE from professional translators with no experience in PE. Although the professionals' PE experience is not extensive and although the results are not statistically significant, they are still indicative of the importance that experience can play in the effort required during PE. It is our intention in the future to build on this research by increasing sample sizes and target languages and by complementing the results with a qualitative analysis of the final translation and post-edited products in order to ascertain if (and how) quality is affected. In addition, we aim to study whether translation experience and areas of specialization and expertise may affect the results.

Acknowledgments

The authors would like to thank the HUBIC Lab at the Athena Research Center in Athens where all the experiments were carried out.

References

Balling, Laura and Michael Carl. (2014). Production time across language and tasks: A large scale analysis using the CRITT translation process database. In John W. Schwieter and Aline Ferreira (eds), *The development of translation competence: Theories and methodologies from psycholinguistics and cognitive science*. Cambridge Scholars Publishing, pp. 239–268.

Besacier, Laurent and Lane Schwartz. (2015). Automated translation of a literary work: a pilot study. In *Proceedings of the Fourth Workshop on Computational Linguistics for Literature* (Denver, CO), pp. 114–122.

Carl, Michael. (2012). Translog – II: A program for recording user activity data for empirical reading and writing research. In *Proceedings of the 8th international conference on language resources and evaluation*, European Language Resources Association (ELRA).

Carl, Michael, Barbara Dragsted, Jakob Elming, Daniel Hardt and Arnt Lykke Jakobsen. (2011). The process of post-editing: A pilot study. In *Proceedings of the 8th international NLPCS workshop –*

Special theme: Human-machine interaction in translation. Copenhagen Studies in Language 41. Samfundslitteratur, Copenhagen, pp. 131–142.

Carl, Michael, Silke Gutermuth and Silvia Hansen-Schirra. (2015). Post-editing machine translation: Efficiency, strategies, and revision processes in professional translation settings. In Aline Ferreira and John W. Schwieter (eds) *Psycholinguistic and cognitive inquiries into translation and interpreting.* John Benjamins, Amsterdam, pp 145–174.

Castilho, Sheila, Joss Moorkens, Federico Gaspari, Rico Sennrich, Vilelmini Sosoni, Yota Georgakopoulou, Pintu Lohar, Andy Way, Antonio Valerio, Antonio Valerio Miceli Barone and Maria Gialama. (2017). A Comparative quality evaluation of PBSMT and NMT using professional translators. In *Proceedings of Machine Translation Summit XVI.* Nagoya, Japan.

de Almeida, Giselle. (2013). *Translating the post-editor: An investigation of post-editing changes and correlations with professional experience.* PhD Thesis, Dublin City University.

Densmer, Lee. 2014. Light and Full MT Post-Editing Explained. http://info.moravia.com/blog/bid/353532/Light-and-Full-MT-Post-Editing-Explained.

Doherty, Stephen, Sharon Brien and Michael Carl. (2010). Eye tracking as an MT evaluation technique. *Machine Translation* 24:1-13.

Elming, Jakob, Laura Winther Balling and Michael Carl. (2014). Investigating user behaviour in post-editing and translation using the CASMACAT workbench. In Sharon O'Brien, Laura Winther Balling, Michael Carl, Michel Simard and Lucia Specia (eds.) *Post-editing of machine translation.* Cambridge Scholars Publishing, Newcastle.

Flanagan, Marian and Tina Paulsen Christensen. (2014). Testing post-editing guidelines: how translation trainees interpret them and how to tailor them for translator training purposes. *The Interpreter and Translator Trainer* 8(2):257–275.

Garcia, Ignacio. (2011). Translating by post-editing: Is it the way forward? *Machine Translation*, 25(3): 217-237. http://www.jstor.org/stable/41487495

Gaspari, Federico, Antonio Toral, Sudip Kumar Naskar, Declan Groves and Andy Way. (2014). Perception vs reality: Measuring machine translation post-editing productivity. In *Proceedings of AMTA workshop on post-editing technology and practice.* Vancouver, pp. 60–72.

Genzel, Dimitriy, Jakob Uszkoreit and Franz Och. (2010). Poetic Statistical Machine Translation: Rhyme and Meter. In *Proceedings of the 2010 Conference on Empirical Methods in Natural Language Processing*, MIT, Massachusetts, pp. 158–166.

Green, Spence, Heer, Jeffrey and Christopher D. Manning. (2013). The efficacy of human post-Editing for language translation. In *Proceedings of the SIGCHI Conference on Human Factors in Computing Systems (ACM).* Association for Computing Machinery, 439-448.

Greene, Erica, Tugba Bodrumlu and Kevin Knight. (2010). Automatic analysis of rhythmic poetry with applications to generation and translation. In *Proceedings of the 2010 Conference on Empirical Methods in Natural Language Processing*, Cambridge, MA, pp. 524–533.

Groves, Declan and Dag Schmidtke. (2009). Identification and analysis of post-editing patterns for MT. *MT Summit XII – The twelfth Machine Translation Summit International Association for Machine Translation hosted by the Association for Machine Translation in the Americas.* Association for Machine Translation in the Americas, pp. 429-436.

Guerberof, Anna. (2009). Productivity and quality in MT post-editing. In Goulet MJ et al. (eds.) *Beyond translation memories workshop.* MT Summit XII, Ottawa. Association for Machine Translation in the Americas.

Jones, Ruth, Ann Irvine. (2013). The (un)faithful machine translator. In *Proceedings of the 7th Workshop on Language Technology for Cultural Heritage, Social Sciences, and Humanities.* Sofia, Bulgaria, pp. 96–101.

Hu, Ke and Patrick Cadwell. 2016. A comparative study of post-editing guidelines. In *Proceedings of the 19th annual conference of the European association for machine translation*, pp. 346–353.

Hvelplund, Kristian Tangsgaard. (2011). *Allocation of cognitive resources in translation: An eye-tracking and key-logging study.* PhD thesis, Copenhagen Business School.

Jia, Yanfang, Michael Carl and Xiangling Wang. (2019). How does the post-editing of neural machine translation compare with from-scratch translation? a product and process study. *The Journal of Specialised Translation* 31:60–86.

Koponen, Maarit. (2016). *Machine translation post-editing and effort: Empirical Studies on the post-editing effort.* PhD Thesis, University of Helsinki.

Koponen, Maarit. (2012). Comparing human perceptions of post-editing effort with post-editing operations. In *Proceedings of the 7th workshop on statistical machine translation.* Montreal, Canada.

Krings, Hans P. (2001). *Repairing texts: Empirical investigations of machine translation post-editing processes.* Geoffrey S. Koby (ed.). Kent, Ohio: Kent State University Press.

Lommel, Arle and Donald A. DePalma. (2016). *Europe's leading role in Machine Translation: How Europe is driving the shift to MT.* Technical report. Common Sense Advisory, Boston.

Mesa-Lao, Bartolomé. (2013). Introduction to post-editing - the CasMaCat GUI. http://bridge.cbs.dk/projects/seecat/material/hand- out_post- editing_bmesalao.pdf.

Mesa-Lao, Bartolomé. (2014). Gaze behaviour on source texts: An exploratory study comparing translation and post-editing. In Sharon O'Brien, Laura Winther Balling, Michael Carl, Michel Simard & Lucia Specia (eds.), Post-editing of Machine Translation, 219–245. United Kingdom: Cambridge Scholars Publishing.

Mitchell, Linda. (2015). *Community post-editing of machine-translated user-generated content. PhD thesis.* Dublin City University.

Moorkens, Joss. (2018). Eye tracking as a measure of cognitive effort for post-editing of machine translation. In Walker Calum and Federico M. Federici (eds.) *Eye tracking and multidisciplinary studies on translation.* John Benjamins, Amsterdam, pp. 55-69.

Moorkens, Joss and Sharon O'Brien. (2015). Post-editing evaluations: Trade-offs between novice and professional participants. In İlknur Durgar El-Kahlout, Mehmed Özkan, Felipe Sánchez-Martínez, Gema Ramírez-Sánchez, Fred Hollowood and Andy Way (eds.) *Proceedings of European Association for Machine Translation* (EAMT) 2015, Antalya, pp. 75–81.

Moorkens, Joss, Antonio Toral, Sheila Castilho and Andy Way. (2018). Translators' perceptions of literary post-editing using statistical and neural machine translation. *Translation Spaces* 7(2): 242-260.

O'Brien, Sharon. (2002) Teaching post-editing: A proposal for course content. In *Proceedings of 6th EAMT workshop on teaching machine translation*, Manchester, UK, pp 99–106.

O'Brien, Sharon. (2007) An empirical investigation of temporal and technical post-editing effort. *Translation and Interpreting Studies (TIS)* 2(1): 83-136.

O'Brien, Sharon. (2009) Eye tracking in translation process research: methodological challenges and solutions. In Inger M. Mees, Fabio Alves & Susanne Göpferich (eds.) *Methodology, technology and innovation in translation process research: A tribute to Arnt Lykke Jakobsen*. Copenhagen studies in language, 38. Samfundslitteratur, Copenhagen, pp. 251-266.

O'Brien, Sharon. (2010). Introduction to post-editing: Who, what, how and where to next. *Paper presented at The Ninth Conference of the Association for Machine Translation in the Americas* (Denver, Colorado 31 October – 4 November 2010).

O'Brien, Sharon. (2011). Towards predicting post-editing productivity. *Machine Translation* 25(3):197-215.

O'Brien, Sharon, Laura Winther Balling, Carl Michael, Michel Simard and Lucia Specia. (2014). *Post-editing of machine translation: Processes and applications*. Cambridge Scholars Publishing, Newcastle.

O'Brien, Sharon and Michel Simard. (2014). Introduction to special issue on post-editing. *Machine Translation* 28(3):159–164.

Plitt, Mirko and François Masselot. (2010). A productivity test of statistical machine translation post-editing in a typical localisation context. *The Prague Bulletin of Mathematical Linguistics* 93:7–16.

Raptis, Spyros and Maria Giagkou. (2016). From capturing to generating human behavior: closing the interaction loop at the hubic lab. In *Proceedings of the 20th pan-hellenic conference on informatics (pci) with international participation*. Partas, Greece: ACM Digital Library, International Conference Proceedings Series.

Sharmin, Selina, Oleg Spakov, Kari-Jouko Räihä, and Arnt Lykke Jakobsen. (2008), Where on the screen do translation students look while translating, and for how long?. In Susanne Göpferich, Arnt Lykke Jakobsen and Inger M. Mees (eds.) *Looking at eyes. Eye-tracking studies of reading and translation processing*. Samfundslitteratur, Copenhagen, pp. 31-51.

Tatsumi, Midori. (2009). Correlation between automatic evaluation metric scores, post-editing speed and some other factors. *MT Summit XII – The twelfth Machine Translation Summit International Association for Machine Translation hosted by the Association for Machine Translation in the Americas*. Association for Machine Translation in the Americas, pp. 332-339.

TAUS. (2016). Taus post-editing guidelines. https://www.taus.net/think-tank /articles/postedit-articles/taus-post-editing-guidelines

Toral, Antonio and Andy Way. (2015). Machine-assisted translation of literary text: A case study. *Translation Spaces* 4(2):241–268.

Vermeer, Hans. (1989). Skopos and commission in translational action. In Andrew Chesterman (ed.) *Readings in translation theory*. Routledge, London, pp.173-187

Vieira, Lucas Nunes. (2016). How do measures of cognitive effort relate to each other? A multivariate analysis of post-editing process data. *Machine Translation* 30: 41-62.

Vieira, Lucas Nunes and Elisa Alonso. (2018). *The use of machine translation in human translation workflows: Practices, perceptions and knowledge exchange*. Report. Institute of Translation and Interpreting.

Vieira, Lucas Nunes, Elisa Alonso and Lindsay Bywood. (2019). Introduction: post-editing in practice – process, product and networks. *The Journal of Specialised Translation* 31:2–13.

Wagner, Emma. (1985). Post-editing systran – A challenge for commission translators. *Terminologie et Traduction* 3:1–7.

Zhechev, Ventsislav. (2014). Analysing the post-editing of machine translation at autodesk. In Sharon O'Brien, Laura Winther Balling, Carl Michael, Michel Simard and Lucia Specia (eds.) *Post-editing of machine translation: Processes and application*. Cambridge Scholars, pp. 2–13.